ISBN number 979-8-9900652-5-3
All rights reserved
Copyright Alan Briggs 2025

The Sabbatical Journey is published by Far Peak Press
No portion of this book may be reproduced without the consent of the author

Portions of this work have been reprinted from Alan Briggs, *Antiburnout: A Lighter Way to Live and Lead in a Heavy World* (Far Peak Press, 2024).

Thank you to my publishing village!
It really does require a team.
Daron Short, cover and tool design
Beryl Glass, layout
Mikelle Mosier, editing
Jonathan Collier, marketing
Quinn Bilodeau, ninja skills
Justin Ochocki, content help

Want to buy a lot of these books or go deeper? For bulk discounts, speaking inquiries or to begin Sabbatical Coaching visit SabbaticalCoachingGroup.com

What people are saying about Sabbatical Coaching

Alan's wisdom helped me transform what could have been just time off into a truly life-changing season. What sets Alan apart is his rare combination of practical experience, spiritual depth, and genuine care. If you're considering a ministry sabbatical, I can't recommend Alan Briggs highly enough.

—Chris, Vermont

A few months before my sabbatical, the quiet whisper I heard from God was "let the land rest". Alan helped me figure out what that meant, ensuring that sabbatical led to sustained fruitfulness on the other side - new steps in my leadership, new staff on our team, and new spaces to expand our ministry.

—Mark, Delaware

They helped us learn how to prepare for it, experience it and reorient back into life after it. It was a game-changer for myself, my family and our church!

—Josh, Louisiana

Working with Alan was instrumental in helping me navigate sabbatical as a season of true surrender rather than just strategic rest. His wisdom and presence helped me embrace the discomfort of slowing down, listen deeply to God, and re-enter ministry with renewed clarity and soul-health.

—Barry, Texas

Alan's guidance and friendship helped me make the most of my sabbatical season—for myself, my family, and my church. It was truly a transformational time in my life, and I'm grateful to God for providing a trusted guide who helped me prepare well, fully embrace the sabbatical, and return with fresh vision.

—Josh, West Virginia

God re-formed my identity during my sabbatical, and Alan was a pivotal part of unlocking that. Now our entire team benefits from a sabbatical framework developed through Alan's coaching and guidance, and our team is healthier—and more productive—than we were before.

—Jesse, Colorado

Sabbatical coaching was a game-changer! I probably would've crashed and burned in a lot of ways, but sabbatical coaching led me through a process to prepare for, experience and re-enter back in.
—Greg, Indiana

the Sabbatical Journey

A field guide to **prepare** for, **experience**, and **reorient** from a life-changing sabbatical

Alan Briggs

To Mom.
You have loved me and so many others
through your work and hospitality.
I have learned to rest, in part,
because you created the space for me to do so.

CONTENTS

PART ONE
Demystifying Sabbatical

Why Do We Need a Field Guide?. 15
What Do We Mean by "Sabbatical"?. 21
What Sabbatical Is… and Isn't 23
The Bruised Narrative of Sabbatical 27
Sabbatical Is Not Nothingness 29
The Bipolar Sabbatical Journey 31
Reflecting on Major Challenges 35
Let's Talk About Burnout 39
Brakes, Alignment and Shocks 43
What Does Sabbatical Have to Do with Sabbath? 47
Rest Requires Trust 55
Wired and Tired. 59
Addicted to Adrenaline 61
The Inhale and the Exhale 63
A Special Note for Pastors 65
A Special Note for Business Leaders 67
Lies We Believe About Sabbatical. 69
Sabbatical Fears 71
Work Is Meaningful 75

PART TWO
The Prepare Phase

The 6 R's of Sabbatical Preparation 85
Three Sabbatical Postures 91
Four Types of Sabbaticals 93
Sabbatical "To-Don't List" 97
Get To's vs Have To's 99
Your Sabbatical Roadmap 101
Your Sabbatical Structure 103
The Sabbatical Thaw 109
The Awkward Process of Requesting a Sabbatical . . . 113
Clarifying Sabbatical with Your Organization 117
Preparing Your Heart 119
Preparing Your Schedule 121
Preparing Your Family 123
Co-Designing Your Sabbatical with Your Spouse . . . 125

Time with AND Away from the Family 127
Preparing Your Mind 129
Preparing Your Team and Organization 131
Your Emergency List 133
Sabbatical Communication Plan 135
The Gentle Boat Ramp 137

PART THREE
The Experience Phase

The First Third: Looking Back. 145
The Fear of Pulling Away 149
Weekly Sabbatical Check-In 153
Caffeine, Alcohol and Exercise During Sabbatical 155
The Fruitfulness of Extended Time Away 159
Assessing Your Tiredness 161
Wins and Disappointments 169
The Second Third: Looking Within 173
Finding a Hobby 179
Zooming Out 181
Impact Goals and Identity Goals 183
The Last Third: Looking Ahead 187
Telling Others About Your Sabbatical 189
Post-Sabbatical Commitments 193

PART FOUR
The Reorient Phase

Gentle Reentry 201
Holding Space to Lead at 80% Capacity 203
Navigating Meetings with Direct Reports 205
The lies about going back 207
Redesigning your schedule 209
Life after sabbatical 211
Sustaining change 213
Creating a sabbatical policy and program 217
Helpful Resources 222
About Sabbatical Coaching Group 223
About the Author 224

PART ONE
Demystifying Sabbatical

Why Do We Need a Field Guide?

"The desperate need today is not for a greater number of intelligent people, or gifted people, but for deep people." [1]
Richard Foster

"*Just keep pushing!*" This is what I told myself every morning as I slid out from underneath the warm covers in the dark. It's what I always did. I learned it from coaches, motivational speakers and an upwardly-mobile culture of achievement. Quitting was never an option. I even saw plenty of cat posters challenging me, "Hang in there!" I'd been hanging in there for years with my claws grabbing onto the branch.

I was writing books that impacted people, getting the invites to speak, and running a business that was supporting my family. I was enthralled with helping those I coach break through barriers, get healthy and create healthy cultures around them. I was even beginning to help leaders navigate their sabbatical for maximum impact. Everything looked great in the impact category, but I was exhausted at the end of each week. Ironic, I know. My energy tank was like an old cell phone that loses battery juice at an alarming rate.

I was doing the things I helped my clients do: taking plenty of time off, making space for the people and activities I love, exercising and sleeping a decent amount. But I couldn't escape the feeling: *"Something is a bit off."* My energy felt like water draining from a hidden leak in a bucket. *"Why am I so tired?"* I would ask myself as I left the office on Fridays. *"Nothing is broken, but something just feels OFF."* Many leaders tell me the same thing. Energy loss is sneaky. It's hard to put a finger on. Questions roll through our minds.

> *Is this what getting older feels like?*
> *Will I always be this tired?*
> *Is this the sacrifice leaders just need to make?*
> *Is this why I get paid the big bucks (or at least better bucks than the rest of my team)?*
> *Will a long break from work even make a difference?*

If you're asking these questions you're in a space Ruth Haley Barton calls "the pre-awareness stage; you know something is not quite right, but you're not sure what it is".[2] If you've ever been there or if you're there right now keep reading.

In recent years we have experienced a massive uptick in sabbaticals for those in spiritual leadership. Pastors, nonprofit leaders and ministry CEOs are increasingly getting the opportunity to experience a sabbatical. Organizations are putting sabbatical policies in place so they become a feature of their culture. As I journey with them they have huge epiphanies about work, family, life, priorities and what truly matters. They come back to their work transformed.

Business leaders are following suit. A 2025 Harvard Business Review article compiled the findings of a Harvard professor who studied over 250 sabbaticals over seven years, including his own. His conclusion: *"I've found that their impact is nearly always transformative."* The summary of the article: *"If you can swing it, the potential payoff is enormous. In fact, taking one could be transformational for your life and career."* [3]

I wish it was that simple: block off the time, go get your sabbatical, climb mountains, stroll beaches, take plenty of naps, magically clarify what matters in life and live how you know you should. Sounds perfect, right? In reality, there are plenty of obstacles to receiving and navigating a sabbatical. Many boards and organizations are afraid to give leaders a sabbatical. Most high-achieving leaders are filled with fear and gnawing questions when they first hear they are up for a sabbatical.

That was me. When it was my turn for my first sabbatical I was *terricited*: overcome by a strange concoction of excitement to be off work and terrified that I would screw it up. Now, a decade later I have witnessed the transformative power of sabbaticals. I have experienced three sabbaticals myself and walked with over seventy leaders through their sabbatical as a sabbatical coach. Going on the sabbatical journey with leaders has become one of the great privileges of my life and vocation. I get a firsthand glimpse at the potential power they hold. When navigated wisely sabbaticals lead to growth, maturity, rest and redesigning life to align with priorities.

> When navigated wisely sabbaticals lead to growth, maturity, rest and redesigning life to align with priorities.

But many people are still terrified of sabbaticals. It seems like some people have a secret code while others have no idea what they do with their time away. It is time to demystify the idea of sabbatical. If a leader does not understand the purpose of sabbatical and clarify a process to wisely walk through their sabbatical that time can even be destructive. With clarity, wise planning and the presence of a sabbatical coach a sabbatical can shape decades of life, ministry and leadership.

You may be a board member, a leader heading on sabbatical, an interested future sabbatical-er or a spouse of someone preparing for sabbatical. I view sabbatical from the inside-out. Before I had read any books on sabbatical I stumbled my way through it twice. As a Leadership Coach a few pastors requested for me to continue coaching them through their sabbaticals. This led to years of deep coaching with leaders and the organizations who wanted support before, during and after their sabbaticals. Leaders replenished during their time away and led differently after their sabbatical. I never sought out to be a sabbatical coach, but we take the role very seriously.

Before we begin this journey together I want to let you know what you're in for.

This is a field guide. This is a practical guidebook for leaders who want to understand and maximize sabbatical. Picture hikers holding a frayed book, looking at maps and reading descriptions of a climb. It's meant to take on some wear and tear as you work through this in some incredible places. I designed this to help you interact with sabbatical up close and personal, not at a distance. If you embrace the sabbatical journey wholeheartedly these pages will be stained with tears and leave a trail of inked epiphanies behind you. God, the designer, is inviting you to design your way forward with Him. Pause to reflect and answer questions. There is no reason to rush! These questions have helped guide many sabbatical sojourners before you. I'll share some references and passages from my book *AntiBurnout* to get a wider perspective on leadership and cultural challenges.

I focus on leaders. I carry a burden for leaders. Many are exhausted, over-extended and fatigued by the weight they're carrying. Leaders feel the weight of constantly making decisions, caring for people deeply and navigating change publicly. When they are healthy others reap the benefits. And, of course, when they are unhealthy, others feel the tremors. Thousands of hours of coaching leaders and consulting with organizations have given me a window to witness how leaders' behaviors cascade down to others. Leaders have a disproportionate influence on the culture. When the leader makes shifts to live healthier and more wholehearted others will benefit and follow suit. This cascade effect is one reason I focus my coaching and writing on leaders. If you do not consider yourself to be a leader you can still glean plenty from this field guide.

Leaders shape the culture. I've seen staff teams following the point leader into exhaustion and chaos. I've also seen healthy staff cultures marked by rest, trust and connection to God. The other day I met a leader who told me, "I was healthier when I left that role than when I began." We need more of that!

My Christian faith guides my understanding of rest and sabbatical. I cannot separate my understanding of rest from the God who designed it. While I often coach leaders and speak to groups who do not share my faith, this guide is focused on leaders with a Christian mindset. This is specifically written for those I coach through sabbatical, spiritual leaders. If you are not guided by the Christian faith and the conviction that God both modeled Sabbath and gave it to humans as a gift it won't soak in quite as deeply.

My aim is to be helpful, not exhaustive. There are plenty of great resources on rest, sabbath and sabbatical. I find leaders who are considering sabbatical or are given a sabbatical need a practical framework to navigate sabbatical. Understanding and stewarding a sabbatical feels overwhelming! This is why I seek to simplify sabbatical, give recommendations for how to maximize it and provide handles to carry transformation into life after sabbatical. My aim, above all, is to be helpful. Our team at Sabbatical Coaching Group wants as many leaders as possible to experience sabbaticals that transform their lives. We love watching leaders reconnect to their families, reprioritize what is important and walk more closely with Jesus.

This content is hard-fought. I'll share real stories from myself and others limping our way through sabbatical and uncovering some incredible things along the way. I'll suggest plenty of steps along the journey birthed directly from coaching leaders through this process. I'll expose you to tools and frameworks to help you organize the chaos in your mind and heart around sabbatical. Ultimately, we hope to give you just enough guidance so you can hear from God and have an incredible experience. Remember, this is a journey, not a checklist.

This is NOT a deep theological treatise on sabbath or sabbatical. Many great resources have been penned on these topics. I encourage you to resist the temptation to learn so much about sabbatical that you fail to experience the gift of sabbatical. Our team at the Sabbatical Coaching group deeply desires for you to have an experience with God during sabbatical, not just to learn more about sabbatical.

This isn't a sabbatical rulebook. We aren't sabbatical pharisees telling you what you are and aren't allowed to do on sabbatical. Every sabbatical journey requires discernment from God and self-awareness about who you are, what you need and the season you find yourself in. You're going to have to hear from God and make some courageous decisions. Let the journey begin!

What Do We Mean by "Sabbatical"?

"A person has to get fed up with the ways of the world before he, before she, acquires an appetite for the world of grace." [4]
Eugene Peterson

There are plenty of different definitions of sabbatical out there. Before we get too far into this guide I want to share the definition of sabbatical I'm working from.

One month or more away from your primary work for the purpose of replenishment with the intention to come back stronger.

Let's break it down.

One month or more. Anything less is a nice vacation. It takes at least a month to begin to thaw out and experience true replenishment.

Away from your primary work. A leader desiring a transformative sabbatical should eject from their main areas of work, but they may need to do side work.

For the purpose of replenishment. This is not designated to complete a project like writing a book or starting a new business.

With the intention to come back stronger. The leader is planning to return to their role or organization, not transition to another one.

Some have used the term sabbatical as a chance to look for their next job, recover emotionally from being fired or take a dream trip or deal with a serious health crisis. These are valid reasons to take a break from work, but they will have a very different effect than the sabbatical definition above. An academic sabbatical often involves extensive research or writing a book. I can assure you writing a book is serious work. Please hear me say I am ALL for taking long breaks from work, shifting gears, receiving medical leave or taking on big projects, but they will have a different focus than the sabbatical I write about in this field guide.

We frame sabbaticals in a unique way that sets them up for major life transformation by way of replenishment. One definition that might be helpful is "renewal leave" (David Alves uses this in his book A Sabbatical Primer). I like that; by leaving your primary work and all its demands we experience fresh perspective and renewal. Sabbatical specialist David Alves says, "A sabbatical is not a vacation. It is a different kind of work - it is a directed time of refreshment and restoration. It is a time for drawing closer and listening more carefully, with the intent of deeper intimacy with God… It is also an intentional release from stressors and overwhelming spiritual and people demands."[5] If you are up for a different kind of work, one that retunes the heart and attends to the health of your soul, keep reading. and change your pace, but please don't quit climbing the mountain in front of you. I'm glad you picked up this book. I've walked with leaders who make changes to their life and leadership and find a healthy, sustainable groove. Yes, it is possible

What Sabbatical Is... and Isn't

In this section I'll help define some differences between sabbatical perception and reality. My aim is not to split hairs here, but to increase clarity and release some weight.

Sabbatical Is a Gift, Not a Reward.
We don't take sabbaticals, we receive them. Our posture and language is very important here. One of God's greatest gifts to his people is rest. We're not talking about getting a few extra hours of sleep, although that's amazing. We're talking about the opportunity to cease striving and enjoy our relationship with God and others.

I believe sabbaticals are a gift from God, but they are often administered through an organization. Most people receive a sabbatical through the direction of a team, board or organization. It's not something you earn, like a performance bonus, it's a gift that's given to you.

Sabbatical Is Engagement, Not Escape.
A big misunderstanding about sabbatical is that it's a giant eject button. Of course, leaders must disengage in certain areas during sabbatical, but it's for the purpose of engaging other valuable areas. Make no mistake, leaders have work to do during their sabbatical, but it's sacred work. It's the work of play, parenting, solitude, prayer,

friendship, listening, travel, rest and reflection. These things aren't a void; they are real things with real benefits.

Sabbatical Is a Hinge Moment, Not a Rest Area.
A sabbatical opens the door to the future. While we may begin sabbatical looking back, a healthy sabbatical naturally lifts our eyes to the future. Sabbaticals have a way of giving us perspective on the past with a clear vision for the pathway ahead. When we make space, God opens our eyes to the world of possibility, of love, of grace. During sabbatical we give God an open invitation to sharpen our blurry vision.

> When we are exhausted we lose vision, but as we get healthy we look forward.

God designed humans to shape the future. When we are exhausted we lose vision, but as we get healthy we look forward. Vision often sharpens for leaders during a moment of sabbatical: a conversation with a friend, a moment looking our child in the eyes, a sunset on the Mediterranean, a bumpy ATV ride with buddies, a quiet moment in a comfy chair, a walk through the neighborhood with our spouse or a happy hour with a friend. Moments shape our stories, and sabbaticals are full of them.

Sabbatical Is a Cosmic Reset, Not a Leadership Hack.
I do not want to cheapen sabbatical or my approach to them. It would've been easier to just create a checklist and forget the guide book and the coaching. But this isn't a leadership hack you follow to get a great result; it's a journey with the living God who invites us to co-design the future with Him.

Sabbatical clears the traffic in our lives, the airspace around us gets quieter and we begin to hear God again. I love this short verse about Moses. *"The Lord would speak to Moses face to face, as one speaks to a friend"* (Exodus 33:11 NLT) During each of my sabbaticals I rediscovered God was my friend. Actually, I realized He was the close friend I stopped calling and hanging out with.

With clear airspace around us during sabbatical our priorities resurface. When we get away from work we realize what truly matters. We realize our minds were distracted, our eyes were diverted, our words were muted, our hearts were numbed and our bodies were distressed. We get to take off the cape and simply be human again. We get the opportunity to notice we have been deformed and pray for the courage to reform the areas that deeply matter.

Sabbatical Is a Creative Pause, Not a Vision Cast.
Most leaders put pressure on themselves to return from sabbatical with something HUGE. Deep down they wonder whether the investment of time, energy, money and others stepping up for them will actually be worth it. *"What will I have to show from my time away?"* they wonder. With an insecure heart, many leaders have gone away with one aim: come back with a massive vision to cast and a strategy to unroll.

In reality it's a pause from the vision casting and the strategy. In this pause many leaders experience a new kind of creativity, the kind birthed from freshness, not pressure. A lack of adrenaline and the absence of checklists yields some of the best "accidental" ideas, innovation and fresh thinking. But it requires the leader trusting the process.

Sabbatical Is a Development Tool, Not a Blank Page.
Sabbaticals may be the best kept secret in leadership development. Why? Lean in a little closer. Are you ready? It forces every team member to grow. It's a planned stress test. Think about it. If everyone needs to rise 10 - 20% to carry the leader's responsibilities while they are gone the capacity of each team member is inevitably going to rise. At the same time the leader is away asking themselves, "Should I be doing everything I'm currently doing?" The leader returns to work with a few tasks that others can and should do instead of them. Incredibly, many of the things team members take on in the absence of the leader are the very things the leader wants to grow out of. Bingo! I've watched this exchange be a gift to both sides.

Sabbatical Is a Relational Reconnection, Not an Isolation Chamber.
One reason leaders fear sabbatical is the idea of isolation. Many get a picture that they are to be completely away from people, journaling and praying eight hours a day, ideally at the nearest monastery for the entirety of their sabbatical. That doesn't exactly sound refreshing to most leaders, especially to extroverts and high achievers. Isolation is not the same as solitude. A wisely planned sabbatical is a combination of meaningful solitude and healthy relational reconnection.

During my recent sabbatical I simultaneously got the alone time I was craving and lots of meaningful time with my friends and family. I needed to pull away in order to reflect, answer some of these questions, hear from God and read things that interested me. I also planned meaningful evenings and day trips with friends, was very present to my family, had an incredible getaway with my wife and planned coffees and lunches with my "Get To" list (more on that later).

> Which of these aspects of sabbatical is most refreshing to hear? Why?
>
>
>
> How can I plan my sabbatical differently in light of these distinctions?

The Bruised Narrative of Sabbatical

The word "sabbatical" has been bruised, and needs to be reimagined. It carries baggage for many. I've heard plenty of stories of leaders who were "put on sabbatical" as a disciplinary measure or even the term they used to quietly fire a leader. This paints sabbatical as something to watch out for, a punishment you do not want. An improper use of sabbatical is the mark of a reactive, untruthful, unhealthy culture. Before sabbatical can be maximized as a health tool we must understand that the story underneath sabbatical is already threatened. We're starting from below ground.

My team and I are trying to reverse the tide. We are delighted to see the rise of sabbaticals as a mark of proactive, healthy cultures. When a sabbatical program is wisely implemented across a staff it becomes a life-altering event and can be seen as a staff benefit. The word gets out. People hear stories of others going on sabbatical, see them come back more grounded and look forward to their opportunity. I've heard plenty of tired leaders wonder whether they could survive sabbatical. They came back grateful, looking forward to the next one.

Some of the most fulfilling sabbatical coaching clients to journey with were the ones carrying sabbatical baggage. We had to re-educate them on what their sabbatical could be before they could embrace it. We had to work hard to shift the narrative. Once they understood why sabbaticals exist and separated it from what they had experienced, they got excited for what was ahead. Dread shifted to anticipation.

> What negative stories or perceptions of sabbatical have influenced me?
>
> How can I reframe those?

Sabbatical is Not Nothingness

"The spiritual atmosphere in which we live erodes faith, dissipates hope and corrupts love, but it is hard to put our finger on what is wrong." [6]
Eugene Peterson

I repeatedly get this question about sabbatical: "What should I actually DO on sabbatical?" Not surprisingly, when high-capacity, fast-paced leaders envision sitting on the couch for a few months in their sweatpants doing nothing, they resist the notion. I don't blame them. It's clear they have the a misconstrued narrative of sabbatical.

Every few months I hear someone talking about rest as "letting the ground lay fallow". This is an Old Testament reference to resting the fields for a year. Whenever leaders hear rest, sabbath or sabbatical framed as fallowness it sounds like a void; a nothingness right now that produces something better later. Letting life and work lay fallow sounds scary to some and boring to others. So, is the soil of our life actually lying fallow during sabbatical? Yes, and no.

My understanding of fallow ground flipped on its head while I was standing in a hot, dusty Arizona field. I was hosting a leadership experience with a group of pastors while a community developer was blowing our minds. He shared the story of their dream of an urban utopia that they brought to life. We stood amidst the fields they protected from development that grew the vegetables we would be eating for our farm-to-table lunch. This was a perfect time to ask for more clarification about the fallow ground concept. "I've heard this concept of letting the ground lay fallow. Do farmers actually do that?" I asked. "Yes, and no," he said with a wry smile. "Let me tell you about cover crops."

Instead of leaving fields empty between growing seasons they actually plant "cover crops". These are real crops like oat, barley, alfalfa, radishes, rye and peas. As they grow they give nutrients back to the soil and increase its fertility. This even helps with erosion, weed control, attracting wildlife and water quality. Mind blown.

Sabbatical is a season of planting cover crops. The field is not empty and barren, it's growing different crops. Sabbatical invites us to work, it's just a different type of work. The work during sabbatical isn't the typical work of sending emails, giving talks, creating reports, making sales and leading meetings. It's a different flavor of sacred work for the heart and soul, work that nourishes us and allows us to continue doing other work. It puts nutrients back into the soil of our lives.

> How does the concept of cover crops give you a fresh perspective on sabbatical?

The Bipolar Sabbatical Journey

I was walking my kids back from yet another trip to the park. I was a few weeks into the disorienting journey of sabbatical, and I felt something I hadn't felt in a long time: bored. I had been walking through the whirlwind of adopting two kids, raising two others and the pressures of pastoring, writing books and coaching leaders. In God's grace I had been given a sabbatical. But on that day it didn't feel like God's grace. It felt like monotony. My mind wandered to how I'd rather be in Fiji with my wife, Julie, instead of pushing a stroller. And then it set in; the good old fashioned feeling of guilt. *"What kind of Dad am I?!? Why am I wishing away this precious time with my kids?"*

Twenty four hours later I experienced something completely different: total engagement with my kids. We were laughing and having a dance party in the living room. My youngest son, Eli, was a Chris Farley look alike at that age, and he loved to shake it! I was fully engaged in dad life and overcome by gratitude for a break from work. It allowed me to be the kind of Dad I wanted to be– undistracted. I fantasized about not going back to work at all. I realized how the demands of people and emails and meetings disconnected me from my kids. And then, the feeling of guilt set in again. *"What kind of pastor am I?!? Why don't I want to go back to caring for the people I love so dearly?"* In just one day my "dad guilt" turned to "leader guilt".

A few weeks later my sabbatical travel heated up. My two boys and I packed up the car and drove across the country staying with friends along the way. It was a parenting highlight reel packed with fun, friends, new places and plenty of laughs. One of our stops was with a friend who lived on a lake. We glided over the glassy water grinning ear to ear as people tend to do on pontoon boats. Everyone is happy on a boat, right? Minutes after exiting the boat my boys and I ran down the dock to a two story platform above the water. After some prodding (and some candy bribes) we all jumped off into the water hand in hand as we screamed out-loud. Picture a pharmaceutical commercial minus the terrifying warnings at the end. We jumped at least a dozen more times. I will never forget that day. It's one of the best memories I've ever had with my boys, and I would've never had it if it weren't for my sabbatical.

The emotions leaders experience during a sabbatical are bipolar and disorienting. Most sabbaticals encase a series of high-highs and challenging lows. Not having work to clock into pulls a rug out from underneath us. We can't disappear from family challenges, we miss the stimulation of meaningful work and we don't get dopamine hits from knocking things off our task list. I also gained a massive respect for stay-at-home parents during sabbatical! I began to fully appreciate the meaningful work God had entrusted to me instead of complaining about it.

I went into that sabbatical mostly blind. I didn't know what to expect. I wish I knew to fully embrace the fun moments without guilt and realize I was completely normal for wanting to go back to work. I wish I would've had a sabbatical coach to process my emotions with. I picture them laughing and reminding me I'm normal and that God is doing precious work inside of me. Sabbatical is a disorienting time of change– arresting leaders from the normalcy of life and inviting them into maturity. It's too important to navigate alone.

Now I get to be the Sabbatical Coach I never had. I help leaders process the good, hard and in-between experiences along their sabbatical journey. I've watched exhausted leaders return to work with vitality and make vital changes to get healthy. I've had wives tell me they got

PART ONE | Demystifying Sabbatical

their husband back during sabbatical. I've watched leaders get clear downloads from God who had struggled to hear anything for years. I've watched dads who struggled to create the time and attention for their kids build it into their schedule. I've had plenty of leaders tell me they needed to resign from their role, only to realize instead they needed to redesign it.[7] Sabbatical is a breathtaking wilderness journey, not a predictable checklist.

Through countless hours of planning sabbaticals, processing them over zoom calls and creating work reentry plans, here's what I've concluded: *when navigated wisely a sabbatical is an incredible tool to transform the priorities, work, family, mental health and future of a leader.*

> Sabbatical is a breathtaking wilderness journey, not a predictable checklist.

What challenges do you anticipate during your sabbatical?

What do you anticipate will be the best parts of sabbatical?

33

Reflecting on Major Challenges

Here are a few of the factors impacting leaders today. You're likely carrying them or pushing through them without even realizing it. Pause to reflect on how they're impacting you.

Weight. If you carry weight on your shoulders in service of others I have great respect for you. You are doing important work in your family, community, business, church or nonprofit. But this weight has real effects.

> How much weight am I carrying right now? (1-10)
>
> Of the things I'm carrying what feels the most weighty?
>
> What effects am I experiencing from carrying those?

Change. We have faced incalculable change in the last decade. Macro changes (like technology, Presidential elections and COVID) and micro changes (like job shifts or the addition of a child) impact leaders internally and externally.

> How much change have I experienced in the last year? (1-10)
>
> Which changes have had the biggest impact on me? Why was that the case?
>
> What side-effects am I experiencing from that?

Pace. Many leaders I interact with are running at an unsustainable pace. Some leaders are responding to the needs of their industry, seemingly winding them up as fast as they will go. Other leaders are shaping the culture from the top down, creating the culture around them. When leaders dial up the speed, others in the organization naturally think, "This is what it takes to succeed and keep up around here."

> How fast has my pace been in the last year? (1-10)
>
> What are others in my organization saying about my pace? (Have I received feedback about my pace or do I need to ask?)
>
> How does my pace impact my team or organization?

Mental load. We are carrying a lot in our brains these days. How can we possibly hold all the details, remember all the things, answer all the emails and make all the decisions thrust at us?!? We must realize we simply cannot do all the things while remaining present and healthy. I am hearing an increasing use of terms like *overload, overwhelm, mental*

PART ONE | Demystifying Sabbatical

load and the corresponding need for mental rest, space and margin. We are longing for what A.J. Swoboda calls, "psychological shalom." [8]

> How much mental load have I been carrying in the last year? (1-10)
>
> What things feel mentally heavy right now?
>
> What areas feel like they contain more details than I can keep straight?

Let's Talk About Burnout

"Can we live at peace with ourselves so that we get out of the fast lane and actually overcome the tendency to respond to life as if it were one long emergency?" [9]
Archibald D. Hart

We live in a burnout culture. It has become a normal part of leadership culture in business, nonprofit work and in the church. In his book *The Burnout Society*, researcher Byung-Chul Han describes our culture as "an achievement society, in which the master himself has become a laboring slave." [10] Almost every profession and niche of society is tangled up with burnout. Han defines burnout as *"voluntary self-exploitation."* [11]

Two other researchers give their own troubling definitions of burnout:

"*A syndrome of emotional exhaustion and cynicism that occurs in individuals who do 'people work' of some kind.*" [12]

"*A chronic state of feeling overworked, overwhelmed and exhausted.*" [13]

Does this sound familiar? Perhaps you've never burned out, but you're living in a constant state of overwhelm. It turns out, it's not just impacting Western culture.

The Japanese have language for the staggering effects of overwork they're experiencing. Their language is far more descriptive than ours.

Shachiku: corporate livestock
Kaisha no inu: dog of the company
Karōshi: death by overwork

The Korean language uses the word, *Gworosa* to describe *"working yourself to death."* Koreans now work more hours per year than almost any other country in the world. Suicide rates have tripled since 1990. For a deep dive on the issues and opportunities of margin I highly recommend the book *Rest* by Alex Soojung-Kim Pang. [14]

Burnout can feel like a distant problem to those out *there:* the CEOs and tech startups sleeping under their desk. But what about "the rest of us"? We're not running large companies or managing a few hundred employees. Those in "people work" are particularly vulnerable. Ministry expert Dr. Wes Bevis created an equation that puts us square in the middle of burnout danger:

Dealing with people + being responsible for favorable outcomes = burnout risk zone[15]

I love the work of communications professor Dr. Arianna Molloy in her book *Healthy Calling*. Her research uncovered those who feel a sense of calling about their work have a much larger burnout risk and find it harder to recover from burnout. If we feel God designed us for this work and it serves people in meaningful ways burnout is more than a career redirect–it can be an identity crisis. One of the healthiest things you can do before sabbatical begins is to look at the burnout epidemic face-to-face and take an honest assessment of your life.

> If I were going to burn out how would I do it? **I'm serious - write down your burnout plan...**

PART ONE | Demystifying Sabbatical

How significant is my burnout risk right now? (1-10)

What area of my work creates the most exhaustion or drain? Why?

What is one small step I can take to limit my exhaustion?

Brakes, Alignment and Shocks

I was close to the end of a beautiful sabbatical. My mind was clear, my stress levels were low and my anticipation for the months ahead was high. I was driving to meet some friends for dinner on a chilly night, and I saw a sign on an auto shop that read, *"Brakes, Alignment, Shocks"*. I chuckled. That's exactly what the gift of sabbatical had given me: new brakes, new alignment and new shocks.

Brakes. During a sabbatical we learn to slow down from our frenetic pace. During this cosmic pause almost every leader says, *"I had no idea how fast I was going."* This speed tends to end poorly for us and those around us. We walk in the front door spun up from work, we answer emails on the way to the bathroom and we crash into the weekend. Most leaders like who they are becoming on sabbatical way more than who they were while they were working. Their spouses usually agree. Sabbatical gives the leader a chance to turn the speed button down on the leadership treadmill and dream about living at a slower pace when they return.

> What has my pace been over the last year? (1-10)

Alignment. We hit potholes in life and leadership. We don't even realize we've taken on incremental damage, and we're driving through our lives off kilter. Something is "off", but we're driving through our lives so quickly it's hard to notice it. We drift to the side of our lane, and our smooth driving has turned choppy. Sabbatical helps the leader realign with their priorities. They can return to work with perspective, priorities and a new found smoothness.

> What area of life or leadership feels misaligned right now?

Shocks. Challenges are inevitable. Bumpy roads are part of life. The question is not if they will happen, but how will we respond when they happen. Conflict, loss and change are a few occupational hazards for every leader. During a sabbatical a leader often gains a new grounded-ness to face the bumpy roads. A replenished leader has a new capacity to absorb the bumps that once shook them. These new shocks don't negate the bumps and potholes, but they limit their impact.

> What small bumps are impacting me more than they should?

After my recent sabbatical I returned to a few painful "surprises". While I didn't expect them, I didn't spin up, stress or blame anyone. I took the bumps as they came, and gathered our team to create solutions. In that moment, I saw the gap between the old me and the new me. One coaching client recently told me, "I'm completely different after sabbatical. It's not like everything is perfect, but I'm responding to the issues with ease". Leaders commonly tell me they have learned to slow down and lead smoother after sabbatical. Their teams are "with" them instead of trailing behind them. Many leaders realize during sabbatical that they accidentally structured their work to exhaust them. They are misaligned. They name these areas and work to redesign their tasks and schedule in a way that is more aligned to who they are. These are some of the natural results of taking our leadership car in the sabbatical shop and getting new brakes, alignment and shocks.

> Which areas of life or leadership do I want to be different after I return from sabbatical?

What Does Sabbatical Have to Do with Sabbath?

"Sabbath is a scheduled weekly reminder that we are not what we do; rather, we are who we are loved by." [16]
A.J. Swoboda

In my late twenties I came to the end of myself. I had talent and drive, but life simply required more than I knew how to give. I had two young, adopted kids and new opportunities at work. Turning up the dial a little higher wasn't working anymore. Out of sheer exhaustion, I uncovered the only path forward; a weekly sabbath. Here's the embarrassing part; I was a pastor. I had told plenty of people it was a good idea, and I had dabbled in it, but I finally surrendered to it.

My wife has always been better at resting than me. It took me a while to catch up to her. These days gave my wife and I one big exhale. We allowed ourselves to breathe deep, take in beauty and enjoy good things. I tried to keep them free from email, work tasks and commitments. On these beautiful days my optimism rose, and my stress receded. I felt more connected to my wife and kids, and I was more pleasant to be around (my wife verified this). I realized I had needs, and I paused to meet them. I also began producing more and better work. My thinking was clearer, and I felt more purpose in my work.

This has been my regular practice for many years now. On my Sabbath day I remember I'm a human again, not just a leader and certainly not a machine. On Sabbath days the cappuccino tastes better, the sun seems warmer, the couch feels cozier, and my priorities are more focused. As leaders and parents we get stuck in the "have-to's" of meeting everyone's needs. We rarely pause and savor the "get to's". Sabbath is a "get-to" day in a "have-to" world.

Sabbath has a rich history. God rested from creating the world not because He needed it, but because He knew we would. He was modeling it for us. Then the Israelites, who were enslaved to Egypt, followed suit taking one day to rest from their grueling labor. Both the principle and practice of Sabbath have sustained the Jewish people for millennia.

> If we want to produce great work we must learn the art of resting well.

This old practice is a breath of fresh air in our anxiety-driven, white-knuckle, go-til-you-drop culture. If you wait to rest until you have the time, you'll never do it. In our culture, we work until we can't anymore. Then we crash. Resting is not crashing. When we get into this work/crash cycle we have nothing left to offer our families and communities. If every week ends at minus five then a great weekend only gets us back up to minus one. We're still living at a deficit. Then we do it on repeat week after week. This cycle has us perpetually living on defense. Until we view rest as essential to life we will continue to over-work.

We must change the paradigm from resting from work to working from rest. Rest is essential to life, to work and to being human. It is possible to live at or below your capacity each week, get true rest, and be ready to take on another week. If we want to produce great work we must learn the art of resting well.

Please know I'm a fellow struggler here. I've run myself ragged several times, and I still resist rest sometimes. I understand what a full life feels like. On a normal week you'll find me running businesses, driving my kids to evening activities, showing up for my friends, squeezing in runs to the grocery store, taking on new projects and making time for hobbies. My wife works a very demanding job, and we share family responsibilities. I am trying to seize these precious years with my four kids. I want to steward my responsibilities, serve others well, and be emotionally available to my family. Like you, if I don't fight for rest, it won't naturally appear. I want you to experience a sustainable life, not the weight of unrealistic expectations. I want to be clear. Here's what I believe about rest.

Resting is not inaction, it is a powerful action.
Resting is not a bonus, it is a necessity.
Resting is not escape, it is engagement.
Resting is not a waste, it is wisdom.
Resting is not selfish, it is caring for you and those around you.
Resting is not crashing, it is preparation.
Resting is not an expense, it is an investment.
Resting is not quitting, it is resisting.

A sabbatical is an extension of Sabbath. This concept is foreign to some and familiar to others. At Sabbatical Coaching Group we define a sabbatical as "a month or more away from your primary work with the purpose of replenishment and the intention to come back stronger." It is usually administered by an organization for a leader to replenish, direct energy into other places and reconnect with their family. Sometimes a person is between jobs or sells their company and designates their own sabbatical season. It usually results in renewed vision for the future. Some leaders dream of a sabbatical, others are terrified by the idea. This time away from work can expose a leader's over-reliance on work and reveal gaps in their identity. When leaders don't plan well for sabbatical it can be destructive, but with some planning it can be a turning point of a person's life, family and leadership. Many leaders have told me their careful planning and wise navigation of sabbatical gave them vision for the next decade of life and leadership. A few have told me it saved their marriage.

I have experienced three sabbaticals at just the right times. These some of the greatest gifts I've ever received. This time away from work allowed me to reconnect with my family, gave my soul space to catch up and helped me lift my eyes to the future. With help from books and others who had experienced a sabbatical, I mustered the best plans I could heading into my first sabbatical. I give my first sabbatical a C–. Years later, I implemented what I learned, and the next one was a C+. I needed a Sabbatical Coach, but I didn't know to look for one. They could've helped me navigate, normalize and learn from the disorientation I was experiencing.

Years later I find myself doing nearly as much Sabbatical Coaching as Leadership Coaching. I get to help leaders plan before a sabbatical (the Prepare Phase), navigate the joy and disorientation of sabbatical (the Experience Phase) and transform their life rhythms as they head back to work (the Reorient Phase).

True rest only happens proactively. If you want to prioritize what matters to you and do excellent work–learn to rest. Time away from work, whether it's two days or two months, gives us the space to re-examine our priorities as we stop producing. Even if you never take more than a long vacation you can prioritize rest every week. I invite you to create habits of rest that allow you to enjoy life, prioritize your family, and work hard. I promise you, it's possible. [17]

Most Christians I meet have a mild level of Sabbath understanding with a high level of Sabbath skepticism. Before we get any further here is a simple definition of Sabbath.

Sabbath is a day set aside every week to rest from work and striving in order to celebrate God and one another.

God gave this to his people as a gift, and the Jewish people practice it to this day. Sabbatical is not new, but we've forgotten about it. Many believe it's simply not possible in modern life. Others have simply forgotten about the invitation amidst the breakneck speed and demands of our culture. For those in spiritual leadership our work revolves around drawing people toward the way of life in Christ, yet we resist the invitations of life in Christ. On the whole we have missed the beautiful invitation to Sabbath. We have Sabbath amnesia. Swoboda says, "Sabbath forgetfulness is driven, so often, in the name of doing stuff for God rather than being with God. We are too busy working for him."[18] Many times, those in ministry are the most Sabbath-deprived. The demands seem so pressing, so right, so spiritual.

Our exhausted modern world is aching for this ancient practice. Sabbath is not a reward; it's a gift. It's not something we take from God, but something we choose to receive from God. For a full resource unpacking Sabbath I highly recommend Swoboda's book *Subversive Sabbath*.

Some people have a vague understanding of the ancient concepts of rest below Sabbath. The Hebrew term that describes a specific type of rest is *Shmita*. Like many aspects of Sabbath and sabbatical the true life is discovered at the intersection of the spiritual and practical. While originally tied to Israel's land, *Shmita* principles can be applied to life and leadership. The two major aspects of *Shmita* are release and reset.

Release. During sabbatical we release many things: control (or perhaps over-control is the better term), stress, outcomes and our identity being tied to our work. We are carrying so much– far more than we realize. When we simply pause and cease striving we realize all the things on our minds from day-to-day. One of the great gifts of my three sabbaticals has been releasing the worries and work I was unknowingly carrying. Our overuse must be regulated and curbed or we, like a field, will erode or get sucked dry of our nutrients. This releasing leaves room for a reset.

Reset. Letting the land rest allows space for future growth. I often talk about "dumping out the junk drawer onto the table". You know, that drawer in your home where all the random junk collects. Some of it is useful, and other stuff needs to go straight in the trash. Until we dump our lives out on the table it's hard to realize what needs to go back in the drawer and what needs to get trashed.

This idea of reset lines up closely with the concept of "regenerative agriculture" that is on the rise today. Remember the term "cover crops"? These are different crops that actually put nutrients back into the soil. I have begun using the term "regenerative leadership": leaving intentional spaces for our creativity, passion and vision to replenish so we can reset. During sabbatical many leaders realize their passion and creativity have been waning. They describe "going through the motions" and "being creatively flat". Upon returning to work many leaders experience a resurgence of creativity and passion for their work. Many leaders also make a commitment to receiving a weekly Sabbath after their sabbatical. Can you hear the reset?

Over time, our minds become overloaded and overused, like a computer with too many tabs open and too many programs running in the background. Sabbatical is more than simply turning our computer off; it's more like clearing out all the tabs and running a software update.

> Rest foreshadows heaven, where we can truly and fully rest.

Shmita goes even deeper. A deep soul rest reminds us we are not built solely for work. Rest foreshadows heaven, where we can truly and fully rest. One day Creation will be restored fully. The Jewish people use a rich phrase *tikkun olam* meaning restoring or repairing the world.[19] It is easy to see how the world is broken and needs repairing, but we often forget we are broken and also need release and reset. *Shmita* also involved freeing servants and releasing debts. This is beautiful in and of itself, but it actually released people from slavish cycles of poverty and even reset their economy. We have backed our way into this "voluntary self-exploitation" (as Han calls it) through overwork, *Karōshi* (death by overwork), *Gworosa* (working yourself to death) and just plain exhaustion from doing all the things.

In the midst of our involuntary slavery toward work our souls crave renewal. While we do this to ourselves there is plenty of greed, exploitation and evil beneath capitalism as we squeeze nearly everything for profit. Sex slavery is alive and well in our world today and feeding economies all over the globe from Denver to Dubai. It grieves me that sabbatical is still a rare privilege that is mostly given to those at the top of an organization. It saddens me that many of the poor are required to work so hard to survive that they simply cannot take a day away from their work to rest. The world is not how it should be. We are not living in Shalom.

PART ONE | Demystifying Sabbatical

What areas of brokenness in our world grieve me the most? Why?

In which area do I most desire release from during sabbatical?

In which area/s do I desire a reset?

Rest Requires Trust

If we cannot trust we will not rest. When we rest we trust God will continue to work. We trust God will provide enough for us, our families and the employees who work alongside of us. During a sabbatical we must also trust our coworkers to work well as we rest.

Despite my best preparation and planning, during one of my sabbaticals, my business suffered. I thought it might, but after doing the very best I could I was okay with whatever results we experienced. As I rested deeply during sabbatical my team also got to experience vacations without expectations during part of that time. The break did, indeed impact our bottom line. I ended up having to cut my salary in half for a few months after this sabbatical. We reset priorities, stopped doing a few things and narrowed our focus. Then, a few months later, our business increased rapidly. We began to experience a new level of impact with our clients. My fulfillment also spiked. And, more importantly, I led with a peace, grounded-ness and gratitude I had never experienced.

Something unique, even mysterious, happens when we submit to *Shmita* cycles of restoration. What kind of freedom could we experience if we ran on *Shmita* cycles? What could change if we promoted cycles of rest for ourselves, our families and our organizations? When we rest and release we leave room for our ego and over-control to melt away and our imagination to reset. We pull up from what feels so urgent and important to taste what our souls deeply desire– rest and reconnection with God and others. When we rest we unearth what truly matters. Rest is the ultimate craving within us, but the thing we think we do not deserve and we cannot handle.

> Rest is the ultimate craving within us, but the thing we think we do not deserve and we cannot handle.

During Sabbath and sabbatical leaders experience a fresh scent of freedom. During their sabbatical journey many leaders are released from the tyranny of work into a gentler and more joyful way to work. As they pull away from work they are pulled deeper into the love of God. Many leaders tell me, "I realized God loves me for me; not for what I do for Him." They stumble into this simple, and deeply profound truth. And they experience freedom. To experience God's love is to experience freedom. It is central to who God is. It was also central the mission of Jesus. Look at these descriptions of the mission of Jesus and the work he came to do.

> *The Spirit of the Sovereign Lord is on me, because the Lord has anointed me to proclaim good news to the poor. He has sent me to bind up the brokenhearted, to proclaim freedom for the captives and release from darkness for the prisoners, to proclaim the year of the Lord's favor and the day of vengeance of our God, to comfort all who mourn, and provide for those who grieve in Zion—to bestow on them a crown of beauty instead of ashes, the oil of joy instead of mourning, and a garment of praise instead of a spirit of despair. They will be called oaks of righteousness, a planting of the Lord for the display of his splendor.*
> (Isaiah 61:1-3 New International Version)

That is *Shmita*. When we rest, God works. God mends our broken hearts, releases captives, comforts the mourning, restores our joy and releases us from our despair. And through all of that God shows us his splendor. As we find freedom through rest it cascades to others around us. As we rest we slow down enough to receive God's love,

PART ONE | Demystifying Sabbatical

grace and gentle restoration. In short, sabbatical is a miraculous space of transformation for broken and exhausted humans.

Your Trust List

Sabbaticals require trust. You have real fears that you'll have to deal with head on. You are surrendering control to God and others. The act of naming these areas is the beginning of the beautiful descent of sabbatical and the growth you will experience. Get very specific about the areas and ways you will need to trust God.

I will have to trust God in these specific ways during my sabbatical...

Wired and Tired

Our minds, schedules, bodies, hearts and souls are working harder than we realize. Perhaps the two things that most characterize leaders today are overly-connected and exhausted. In short, leaders are wired and tired.

Over the last few decades the rise of hyper-availability has deeply impacted the role of work, especially for the leader. Screens are wearing us down. As long as our screens are on, we are "on". We're never more than a moment away from a buzz or ding where someone gives us another demand. We are WAY to available. Most leaders can be reached through five or more methods. Not long ago you had to call a work phone during the day and get past a receptionist to speak to a leader. Our hyper-connectivity makes disconnection more challenging than ever but also more rewarding than ever.

There is a sneaky tiredness under the surface of most leaders' lives. We're always more tired than we think. Think you're okay? You're probably tired. Think you're tired? You're probably exhausted. Think you're exhausted? You might be heading toward burnout. When a leader pauses for an extended break they realize just how wired and tired they are. Sabbatical allows leaders to find space away from the screens that signal our demands. The adrenaline drops, people stop calling you to solve problems, auto-responder creates a dam for the flood of emails and you gain much-needed perspective on your life.

The Sabbatical Journey

I get the joy of watching sabbaticals do their work. They are an incredible tool to slow a leader down and expose them to the things that are challenging to notice in the midst of the whirlwind. When a leader intentionally lets go they gain valuable perspective. After a well-planned sabbatical I see leaders becoming more present to God and their families, trading pressure for joy and feeling the freedom to become more at home with themselves.

> How does technology complicate or pressurize my life?
>
> Which communication channel causes me the most stress or pressure?
>
> What would becoming more at home with myself look like?

Addicted to Adrenaline

"Don't underestimate the value of doing nothing."
Winnie-the-Pooh

Many leaders are experiencing something physiological going on below the surface. For centuries many Christians have had an underlying mistrust of the body and science. Over the last decade we've been waking up to effects of the body and mind over-functioning and overloading. At the same time research in this area has exploded. So have our connection inputs and screen time. Nearly every leader I meet admits to being deeply affected by increasing demands, decision fatigue and information overload.

One of the early practitioners to apply science to ministry was Archibald Hart. He has been warning leaders of the adverse effects of adrenaline for decades. He says, "For some of you, adrenaline management will mean unlearning an addiction to your own adrenaline; you may have become so dependent on the high your adrenaline supplies that you may have difficulty giving it up." [20] Many leaders experience a surprising crash at the beginning of their sabbatical due to this dip in adrenaline.

As I prepared for my first sabbatical I realized I was living too fast and too caffeinated. I decided to go cold turkey off caffeine. I anticipated the impact there, but the bigger impact was weening off my adrenaline dependency. Adrenaline is sneaky, and impossible to quantify. Strangely, we can become addicted to this fight or flight internal drug that keeps us living fast. Hart says, "It is easy to see why many become addicted to a state of high arousal. The feelings of security it provides can give us a dangerously false sense of well-being." [21] This is far more dangerous than we realize. This drug is cheap, easy to find and hard to detox from.

Stress is literally killing us a little bit at a time. It is not reserved for emergencies, major work deadlines or those with a gaggle of young kids. Hart adds,

> By far the greater amount of stress damage today is brought about not by major life traumas, but by agreeable experiences, exciting challenges or stimulating competition... Leadership attracts Type A people; those of us who like a serious challenge and get a rise from achieving big things. This can define us as impatient and lacking contentment. Some other characteristics of type A people: *competitive, easily irritated by delays, low tolerance for frustration, hard-driving and ambitious, aggressive, easily angered, cannot relax without feeling guilty, confident on the surface but insecure within.* [22]

Sound familiar?

In what ways do I live off adrenaline in my weekly schedule?

Which of the above characteristics do I most identify with?

The Inhale and the Exhale

*"Without a rich theology of labor,
we'll have an impoverished theology of rest."* [23]
Mark Buchanan

The life of the leader is pointed outward much of the time. Our eyes are looking at others making sure they have what they need. We are naturally drawn to solving problems, caring for those who hurt, covering for those who need a break and getting our families what they need all while keeping the bank account full. We often neglect to care for ourselves and those we love the most. We give speeches and sermons that we often contradict, despite our best intentions. The expectations and responsibilities are heavy. The cobblers kids are wearing flip flops in the snow.

Leaders are constantly exhaling for others. We often aren't inhaling enough fresh air to keep this cycle going. Sabbath and sabbatical are a chance to breathe in and give ourselves what we need again. It gives us a chance to not be a leader, to simply be human-sized again (I borrowed this idea from my friend and author Steve Cuss).[24] The expectations to do all the things make us feel like we need to be a superhero to simply get through the day. Leaders get to breathe deep on sabbatical and focus back on things that matter most, but we may have prioritized the least.

What practices help me inhale the life I need in order to serve others?

What happens in me when I don't inhale these but continue to exhale for others?

A Special Note for Pastors

"*How long does it take to develop a mature pastor?*" I asked this to a board who was considering gifting their pastor a sabbatical. The board chair responded "Thirty seven years." That's how old their Lead Pastor was. Touché.

I've concluded it takes around twelve years to develop a mature pastor to effectively lead a church in the West. Yet we can lose a pastor in twelve months of strain and burden. There are growing concerns about the "pipeline of pastors" drying up. I see this as well. But here's one thing we can do: protect the ones we've got. If you are a board member or committed congregant reading this I encourage you to help build systems that will cultivate longevity for your whole pastoral team. David Alves says, "Pastoral fatigue and burnout cost the church more than just money; they cost lives, drying up the pastoral pool…Congregations often don't realize how much it costs them in terms of broken lives, time wasted and money squandered in the years it takes to select and replace pastors."[25] When you think about sabbatical, I encourage you to see it as an investment, not an expense. You are investing in the long-term growth of your pastors and the long-term maturity of your congregation. This hits close to my heart.

I served as a pastor for thirteen years. Then I transitioned to coaching leaders. Many of them are pastors. As I stepped away from the day-in-day-out pressures of pastoring they became more clear. I saw the ministry forest from a nearby hill instead of looking up at the canopy from below. There are plenty of high expectations for pastors being a model citizen, walking with congregants through high and low moments, loving their families well and being an informed leader in an increasingly-post-Christian culture. The pressure is immense.

Pastors have an extra dynamic most professions won't experience; producing nourishing spiritual content on a regular basis. This is one significant weight of pastoring. Pastors read the Bible as both a personal guidebook and a text book to teach their next lesson. The result is often needing to exhale amazing sermons, Bible studies and staff talks while inhaling fresh thoughts from God. Many pastors tell me they view sabbatical as a chance to open the Bible simply to hear from God, to inhale, instead of crafting their next sermon. Constantly being on the stage with the need to "feed the content beast" steals joy and diminishes creativity. In some ways the pressure of producing content has gone down and in other ways it has gone up.

> Too much stage with too little time to hear from God deforms a pastor. Sabbatical is one tool to re-form pastors.

The rise of teaching teams is wise and incredibly encouraging to see. Many pastors are taking more time off. A growing number of pastors take a month off in the summer for vacation and study to recalibrate. Too much stage with too little time to hear from God deforms a pastor. Sabbatical is one tool to re-form pastors.

Over the last few decades the expectations for excellent sermons have skyrocketed. Many church attenders listen to multiple sermons throughout the week from pastors across the country. Many of them are world-class communicators. Pastors also feel the weight of knowing their sermon may be streamed by many more people at a distance than are joining in the room. These pressures make sabbatical an incredible exhale for pastors to just be humans and inhale full breaths of life so they can continue exhaling as they serve others.

A Special Note For Business Leaders

You may find yourself saying, "You don't get it. Church or nonprofit leaders can schedule a Sabbath every week or build in sabbaticals, but not those of us in business. There is no way!" I hear you. I coach business leaders and owners, and I run a few businesses myself. The demands are high to continue producing, especially on those in service industries.

I've had the honor of working with owners after they sell their business to reimagine what is ahead. In the strange post-exit season money is high, uncertainty is high and meaning is often low. There's a low-grade confusion that few can understand in this moment. Many choose to receive a sabbatical season away from work, although few call it that, to reevaluate their desires and redesign their life. I love coaching leaders through this season to reimagine what's ahead. I also love hearing how they grow, mature, find meaning and build in sustainable rhythms on the other side of this. I challenge you to build in rest now as you build the company or before you sell it. You don't have to ride the rocket for years to get rest every week or an extended rest season.

While the challenges you face are slightly different, the principles in this field guide will yield the same results for you. The same invitation for rest awaits you. Also, the same effects will hit you and maybe even your business if you do not build in rest and recovery before it's too late. Business owners can learn a lot from those experiencing sabbaticals in other fields while working around the unique challenges rest may present to those in your field. Plenty of businesses and even corporations are building in sabbaticals to combat burnout, increase retention and boost creativity. Harvard Business Review reported how sabbaticals are on the rise among business leaders [26] and I believe we will see a huge uptick in business sabbaticals in the next decade. While the focus of this book is more on ministry and nonprofit leaders I want to challenge you to lead the way by modeling a weekly Sabbath and getting creative to plan your sabbatical.

I have to mention ChickFila here. The blue signs on interstates advertise food options for the upcoming exit reminding us of only one that is "Closed Sunday". They are thriving, perhaps even exploding, yet they take every Sunday off. The question is, "Are they thriving partially BECAUSE they take Sunday off?" It's a fascinating study. They've changed the landscape of business by how they treat customers and employees and by their audacious decision for their buildings to remain dark and closed 14% of the week.

Lies We Believe About Sabbatical

*"It is well said in the old proverb,
'a lie will go round the world while truth is pulling its boots on'."* [27]
Charles Spurgeon

Before we are ready to receive the gift of sabbatical we must identify our lies about it. I realize views on sabbatical vary. You may be sabbatical-skeptical, sabbatical-curious or sabbatical-pumped as you read this. People land all over the map in their emotions regarding sabbatical. Even if sabbatical is a healthy thing in your organization you'll need to continue to remind people why you support it. People are forgetful and new employees or board members may have no previous sabbatical knowledge. Here are some common lies people often believe about sabbatical.

The leader is (secretly) leaving after sabbatical. This is different from a transition time or being given space to look for a job. Our team won't coach leaders if we get wind they are secretly disguising an organizational exit with a sabbatical; that's deception. We want the leader to come back stronger, wiser, sharper and ready for what's ahead.

Sabbatical is for leaders who are sick or have had moral failures. Sabbatical is for the healthy, not the sick. Disciplinary leave, medical leave or family leave can be wise moves to care for a leader and cultivate healing for an organization, but they are not the same as a sabbatical.

The Sabbatical Journey

Sabbatical is a long vacation. Most people picture a margarita in hand on the beach in front of their condo in Florida. While vacation may be a piece of sabbatical, it's not the fullness of it. I encourage a few weeks of sabbatical to be dedicated to vacation and the other weeks intentionally designated to other pursuits. Sabbatical is engagement, not escape.

The leader won't be able to cut it after sabbatical. Plenty of people have a belief before, and even during a sabbatical, that they will not be able to lead at the same level after sabbatical. It's like a young, healthy NFL player believing if they pause for a month to recover after the season they won't be able to run, pass or cut like they did last season. The recovery time actually thrusts them forward. Also, remember NFL careers are short, except for Tom Brady, while our work careers require decades of sustained energy and reinvention.

> Which of these lies have I believed about sabbatical?
>
>
> How have the lies impacted my view of sabbatical?

Sabbatical Fears

"Rest is a daunting proposition when you've worked for everything you have." [28]
Saundra Dalton-Smith, M.D.

Everyone has fears about sabbatical. Everyone. These gnawing fears can cause leaders to avoid sabbatical for years. There is a polarity to sabbatical, a push and pull. Most leaders long for time away from work, but struggle to make it happen. I have no doubt these fears are responsible for many leaders delaying a sabbatical for decades or until they hit retirement. I'm glad leaders have this fear as long as it doesn't dominate them.

This could be a waste of time. This is, by far, the biggest fear leaders acknowledge. Some spin it positive: "I want to be different when I return!" The leaders I work with want to be good stewards of the time their organization has blessed them with. They don't want to waste it. They want their sabbatical to count, to look back years later and say, "That time changed the course of my life!" This is actually a great sign when we excavate below it.

My team can't manage without me. This may be true in areas, but let's flip this around. Here are some helpful questions; "How can I prepare my team for my absence? In what areas do I need to help them grow so I can be away? How much lead time do they reasonably need?" Once we answer these questions we can work to prepare our teams.

I'll miss my work and my team. FOMO is real. If you love what you do, and the people you work with, you'll likely experience this. It's a great problem to have. You'll have to be honest, hit this head on and realize you will come back with even more gusto for your work. Sabbatical helps leaders stay in love with their work for a long time.

I won't know who I am away from work. In a culture of visibility and production it can be terrifying to detach who we are from our public persona and our production. Sabbatical can be an ego gut punch, especially if you are in a forward-facing or public role. It's a chance to hit this identity challenge head on. For many leaders this is the central battle of sabbatical. During sabbatical many leaders realize how attached they've become to their role. They often experience relief when they realize they weren't the sum of what they did at work.

I'll have to deal with uncomfortable things. Yep, you probably will. It's a hard, but healthy, opportunity sabbatical affords us. Chances are those uncomfortable things are even more important than your work. In our culture, work and achievement have become idols, and many of us have become functioning work addicts, medicating ourselves from the dull pain we experience below the surface.

Name Your Sabbatical Fears

Fear:
Why is this scary to me?

Fear:
Why is this scary to me?

PART ONE | Demystifying Sabbatical

Fear:
Why is this scary to me?

Fear:
Why is this scary to me?

Fear:
Why is this scary to me?

Work Is Meaningful

"If God's purpose for your job is that you serve the human community, then the way to serve God best is to do the job as well as it can be done." [29]
Timothy Keller

God designed work to be meaningful. He invites us to co-create with Him. It's part of being made in his image. The Apostle Paul says, *"We are His work. He has made us to belong to Christ Jesus so we can work for Him. He planned that we should do this."* (Ephesians 2:10 New Living Version) We are work. And we have work to do.

We forget the work many of our biblical heroes did every day. Joseph was the COO of Egypt. Lydia was a fashion guru. Joshua was a five star general. Daniel was Chief of Staff to the president. We have undervalued the meaning and witness of good work. Martin Luther famously said, *"The Christian shoemaker does his Christian duty not by putting little crosses on the shoes, but my making good shoes, because God is interested in good craftsmanship."* Work is not only meaningful, it is inherently valuable.

We can over-value or under-value work. Work becomes dangerous when it takes center stage in our lives. That's also when it loses its meaning and turns from a blessing to a curse. Swoboda says it this way: "Work is not a mistake or a curse. Yet work becomes our curse when it becomes what we worship." [30] Others under-value work.

Plenty of people talk down about work trying to slide past it and get to the weekend as easily as possible. If we do not see work as meaningful we will be constantly seeking escape from it. Sabbatical gives us a chance to pause our daily work in order to zoom out and get perspective.

Consider Adam and Eve in the garden. They were given the meaningful work of tending to the garden and naming the animals. Meaningful work already existed, but now there was a brand of work called toil; hard work minus the meaning. When we over-work and lose perspective our meaningful work drifts into toil. It's not the work that changes; we change. We drift. We try to work hard to obtain our identity, which never delivers as we hope it will. You can hear the drift in King Solomon's words.

It is useless for you to work so hard from early morning until late at night, anxiously working for food to eat; for God gives rest to his loved ones. (Psalm 127:2 New Living Translation)

This sounds like the leadership treadmill. In our insecurity we scramble, setting the alarm earlier each day to cram more tasks in. We stay up and work a few hours after the kids are in bed so we can start tomorrow feeling good about ourselves. This scramble is driven by the fear of falling behind, failing to produce, falling apart, and not putting enough into the bank account. We lose sight of the gift and purpose of our work as we punch the dial harder and just keep putting one foot in front of the other. It's an exhausting cycle that has claimed us all at some point.

God's great gift is rest. We're not just talking about sleep here, although that is one byproduct of a restful state. We're talking about peace and contentment to breathe deep even when life isn't tidy and tucked in and all our questions aren't answered. Rest reminds us it's okay when everything isn't okay.

For most North Americans Sabbath has remained a distant dream, an unknown reality. It may exist for those "over there" without the kids, the responsibilities or the demands. But the Jewish people have had a very different experience of Sabbath. Hebrew writer Ahad

PART ONE | Demystifying Sabbatical

Ha'am is known to have said, "More than the Jewish people have kept Shabbat, Shabbat has kept the Jewish people." The practice of weekly sabbath is one of the greatest ways the Jewish people have kept their customs and maintained their identity. Like so many of our deep desires, we resist sabbath, yet we so deeply yearn for it.

I can't count how many leaders have told me, "I don't really need as much rest as everyone else." This may sound pompous (or extremely familiar) to you. I actually think they are trying to say something else: "Sitting around just sounds boring - I want more than that." Sometimes we've over-emphasized rest without properly emphasizing good work. The Pharisees lived by the Sabbath command and completely missed the point. Jesus himself said, *"The Sabbath was made to meet the needs of people, and not people to meet the requirements of the Sabbath. So the Son of Man is Lord, even over the Sabbath!"* (Mark 2:27-28, New Living Translation) Or The Message paraphrase, *"Then Jesus said, "The Sabbath was made to serve us; we weren't made to serve the Sabbath. The Son of Man is no yesman to the Sabbath. He's in charge!"*

> Like so many of our deep desires, we resist sabbath, yet we so deeply yearn for it.

The last thing our team wants to do is function like sabbatical pharisees, telling people what they can and cannot do on their sabbaticals. This is not our role. But we do want to remind people of this beautiful gift of Sabbath, and the extension of sabbatical. We invite you to receive the loving invitation from the God behind the Sabbath. I love how medical doctor and author Saundra Dalton Smith says it; "We are not made for rest; rest is made for us. Rest is God's gift back to His people." [31]

Many have suggested: "If you work with your body, sabbath with your mind, and if you work with your mind, sabbath with your body." This has always resonated deeply with me. My work is heavily dependent on my brainpower, with few demands to my body. I create ideas, solutions, content and questions that serve others. This leaves my brain tired at the end of the week. My mind can easily over-engage during the week while my body is under-engaged. My work is also largely intangible; I have no physical object to show for my work like a painter, landscaper or contractor might.

Many years ago I discovered how helpful it was to engage my body during Sabbath. On the weekends I would drift to woodworking, gardening or painting (canvas, not walls. I HATE painting walls!). A long hike is a great rest for my mind. In fact, one of the healthiest things I have done on any of my sabbaticals is investing in my twenty year dream of learning to weld. Whenever I put the welding hood on (the cool looking flip down helmet) I couldn't think about anything other than connecting two pieces of steel. I apprenticed under a welder and stumbled my way into learning the craft a few hours at a time. Immersing myself in a cold stream and moving to the rhythm of my fly rod is a way I get lost in time. I'm so focused on tricking the trout that I can't think of anything else. Experts call it "deep play." I call it a great morning.

When I was a pastor my heart and soul often felt strained at the end of the week. It wore me down to hear how people were being broken and battered by life. I learned to seek out beautiful things like mountain views, visual art or design projects. Tim Keller once said, "Beauty heals the soul." If your soul is tired get to a beautiful place. Colorado feels like cheating—it's easy for me to find a place to look up at Pikes Peak. If you live in a very normal place find a forest path, visit an art gallery or chase a sunset.

Our misunderstanding of what rest is has made so many of us believe we don't even want it. Rest is NOT simply sleeping more or sitting on the couch in sweatpants. That is not a vision that enlivens many leaders. Rest should involve delight at some level, not just crashing. In her book *Sacred Rest* physician Dr. Saundra Dalton-Smith unpacks seven different kinds of rest; *physical rest, mental rest, emotional rest, spiritual rest, social rest, sensory rest* and *creative rest*.[32] Many of these are active and engaging, not passive and boring. As one who feels at home being active in the outdoors and loves working with my hands, creative rest has given me permission to play. Sensory rest has been helpful amidst the overwhelming noise and chaos inherent to a family of six. If we do not increase our imagination of what rest can be we are likely to continue avoiding it. Sabbatical is an ideal spot to learn this.

It turns out rest is one of the most effective ways to work well. In his book *Rest* Alex Pang explores the role of rest in the lives of many people who have shaped our modern world. Many of these innovators and trend-setters had distinct habits of pulling back from work for leisure, relaxation, walks, conversation and even naps. This is what's behind the curtain of many athletes who have performed at a high level for a long time, like Lebron James' sleep habits. Google it. It's not that successful leaders have squeezed rest into their lives, it's more that rest and recovery were big parts of their lives that helped them create great work.

> If we do not increase our imagination of what rest can be we are likely to continue avoiding it.

I recently led a workshop for overwhelmed business leaders who wanted to avoid burnout. They seemed intimidated at the idea of resting, especially on a regular basis. I shared the list below called "Surprising Ways I've Found Rest." Notice how many of mine involve movement and the outdoors.

Woodworking. Saying "No" to extra meetings. Long meals with friends, "just because." Putting my phone to bed at 8PM. Naps. Not checking email until 9AM. Walking a mile on warm nights with my wife. Putting my phone on Do Not Disturb or Airplane Mode. Defining my drains and fills and following those. Hiking mountains. Blocking off a "Think Day" every few months. Hammock breaks. Fly fishing. Hosting fire nights. Listening to Scripture as I move. Welding. A cup of coffee next to my wood stove on a cold Saturday morning. Stretching in the sauna after I work out. Drinks with my wife or friends on the back porch. Saying "no" to almost everything before 1PM on Saturday. Getting near running water. Camping. Mini golf with my kids. Bike rides without goals.

The Sabbatical Journey

List the small ways you find rest

PART TWO
The Prepare Phase

The Prepare Phase

You've already learned a lot about sabbatical, and you've answered some self-assessment questions. Now we turn the corner to actually prepare for your sabbatical. I encourage you not to skip over any tools or questions. Work through these in sequential order. I've never met a leader who regretted their sabbatical preparation.

I continually get asked a question by leaders hoping for a sabbatical, "How long should I prepare before my sabbatical?" While every situation is different and there's no perfect sabbatical, a good rule of thumb is to actively prepare for at least three times the length of your sabbatical. For a one month sabbatical this is three months, but for a three month sabbatical this is nine months. There is a huge correlation between the effectiveness of the sabbatical and the leader's preparation process.

A long runway allows a leader to prepare the team. Proactive sabbaticals create health, while reactive sabbaticals create panic. Some leaders have gone on sabbatical for medical reasons or the birth of a baby. I would rather the organization call this "medical leave" and "maternity/paternity leave." Laying in recovery beds or nursing a new baby isn't exactly designed for replenishment. The Prepare Phase is VITAL to a sabbatical.

I will never forget when a leader called me and told me he had decided to give himself a sabbatical. Ten days later. That's right. He hadn't let his team know yet, but he would be turning operations over to his second in command to run the whole ship. It was a hail Mary play in every sense. It was an emergency move to avoid total burnout, not a true sabbatical. It was a disaster for his business.

Another leader was on the complete opposite end of the spectrum. He planned on a sabbatical, but due to COVID he felt he needed to delay his sabbatical in order to help stabilize the team. He wisely made this choice and delayed his sabbatical eighteen months. He had an incredible sabbatical with big takeaways for his next season of life and ministry. His team did great without him, because they were prepared. During a proactive sabbatical everyone wins.

The 6 R's of Sabbatical Preparation

Here are six big areas to think through, plan for and discuss with your spouse as you prepare for sabbatical. They will impact how your sabbatical unfolds, so it's important to get very clear here.

Recreation: Experiences and moments of fun, enjoyment or creating

It's important to have delightful things you're looking forward to. These range from hobbies to experiences to physical things you want to create. A few of these may happen across the world on a trip, but most of these can happen across town.

If you're married, I encourage you to have an experience you're really looking forward to, an experience your spouse is really looking forward to and an experience you're really looking forward to together. This builds anticipation and allows you to enjoy hobbies separately and together.

> What do I want to create or enjoy during sabbatical? Why?

The Sabbatical Journey

Rest: Replenishment for the body, mind, heart and soul

We're not talking about sleep here, although I hope you get plenty of it. This is more about resting in these four domains so you can begin to replenish. Remember, your body will need to rest and let down first then your mind can let down. This will allow your heart and soul to go through the replenishment process as well.

> Which areas do I need replenishment?
>
> What do I believe is the best pathway to replenishment in these areas?

Reconnection: Areas you would like to grow in or reconnect with God about

The busyness and challenges of life naturally breed disconnection. Many leaders talk about "the drift", where they drift away from the things they love or the spiritual practices that once sustained them.

Maybe you want to be the best parent possible, but you haven't studied parenting in several years. Maybe you find deep connection with God in prayer but it's the first thing to slip from the schedule when life gets full. Maybe you are a pastor and feel the pressure to create a sermonette every time you read the Bible instead of getting to be a curious learner. Identifying an area you want to grow in or a way you want to reconnect with God and others is a great way to prepare for your sabbatical.

> In which areas would I like to learn about or grow in during sabbatical?

> In which areas do I need to reconnect with God?

Relocation: Experiencing new places, even if it's the next town over

One of the great gifts of sabbatical is the space to get into new environments. Our brains think differently when we enter new environments. Mark Batterson often says, "Change of pace + Change of place = Change of perspective." Some people have the resources to take unique or extravagant trips across the globe. Others enjoy finding a condo they can rent or borrow and use that as a basecamp for their family. Others stay close to home and treat it like an in-town vacation. They do day trips within a few hours. Don't believe the lie that you have to get on a plane or cross an ocean to have a meaningful relocation during sabbatical.

I've had a small budget on each of my sabbaticals, so I got creative. One of my sabbaticals featured a monster road trip with my two boys staying with friends across the country. They provided us dinner, a place to sleep and showed us around their town. They treated us like royalty with boat rides, ATV adventures, backyard BBQ's and connections to incredible community leaders. We'll never forget those memories. During my most recent sabbatical I tried to go to as many independent coffee shops as possible. My favorites were little spots in cool towns nestled in the Rockies. One leader I coached loves going to small Texas towns and walking through antique stores. I challenged her to take a day trip once or twice a week to one of those little towns. She had a blast, and didn't have to spend much money.

> Which places can I plan to visit?
>
> How long would I like to visit them for?

Relationships: Investing in family or friends in ways that my normal work impedes

Work takes up so much of our lives that it tends to get in the way of relationships. We fall out of touch with people we love being around. I encourage leaders to save up money for great meals and experiences with friends during sabbatical. I also ask them to consider doing a trip or meaningful activity with someone they've lost touch with. One leader I coached said his fishing trip with his aging father was his sabbatical highlight. The extra space during sabbatical opens the door to take a risk and ask someone to go enjoy an activity together. Others tell me how special it was to take day trips or weekend trips with their kids. Some of my clients let their kids choose the big events they'll do together. They end up doing something they've never done with their kid like a concert, road trip, Nascar race or museum tour.

> How do I desire to invest deeply in my family or friends during sabbatical?
>
> What relationships do I desire to cultivate or rekindle?

Resources: The necessary finances or relationships to meet my sabbatical desires

Ok, now is where we talk about money. We have to. If you want to take your spouse, family or child on a trip it will require money. You're going to need to plan for it.

Many leaders ask me, "How much money is customary for an organization to bless a leader with?" The answers are all over the board. My pastoral sabbaticals didn't include any finances. We had to start saving and get creative for things we wanted to do. It is common for my clients, especially when they lead the organization, to be given an additional month of salary as a sabbatical budget. This is nice because it's a round number and others on staff can receive this in proportion. Boards shouldn't micromanage how leaders utilize this; it's a gift.

Also, this is where sabbatical coaching comes in. When leaders are first getting clearance for a sabbatical I challenge them to ask the board to include sabbatical coaching in their package. This is a GREAT investment for everyone, and it should just be considered part of the sabbatical package. It truly makes everything else go in a smooth and healthy manner during sabbatical. I am also a fan of leaders getting counseling paid for if they desire to pursue it, but I don't think a leader should be forced into counseling. Again, healthy leaders pursue relationships like coaches and counselors to help them get healthy and stay healthy during sabbatical.

It's vital to see any funds associated with sabbatical as an investment, not an expense. If planned for wisely, sabbatical funds will come back to bless the leader, family and organization with huge dividends later.

> What financial or relational resources is my organization providing?

The Sabbatical Journey

> Will they pay for me to receive sabbatical coaching?
>
> What additional resources will I need to obtain?

Three Sabbatical Postures

Each sabbatical is unique, but I observe three different postures leaders have heading into a sabbatical.

Proactive sabbatical posture. This is when sabbaticals are regularly offered ahead of time every several years. Seven years is common, but I like five better. In this posture a leader doesn't have to ask for it; they see it coming, whether they think they need it or not. We love proactive sabbaticals, because these have the greatest chance to create health for the leader, the family and the organization. Leaders often feel like they don't need a sabbatical, but while on sabbatical they realize they were much more tired than they thought. We're always more tired than we think, we just have to pause long enough to realize it.

Responsive sabbatical posture. This is a sabbatical in response to a long season of challenging life or leadership circumstances. Sabbaticals began to rise about a year after COVID began. The strain was getting to leaders. Some leaders have been granted a sabbatical after battling through exhausting family challenges like chronic health issues of a spouse, caring for aging parents or extended struggles with their children. This can be a gift that leads to recovery, but it cannot be planned for as well as a proactive sabbatical.

Reactive sabbatical posture. This is incredibly short-notice, and generally pursued as a last resort. Reactive sabbaticals usually arise from major challenges, and they often create organizational chaos for those around them. I encourage leaders and organizations to label this something other than sabbatical. They can label it as a disciplinary leave, family leave, medical leave, a transition season or even an investigation. If they do not rename these types of leave then they will have a hard time overcoming negative sabbatical stigmas when offering others a sabbatical.

> Which of these postures do I have going into my sabbatical?

Four Types of Sabbatical

Every sabbatical is different. This is how it should be. The life stage, family season and fatigue level impact the leader heading into sabbatical. Sabbaticals are dynamic, not static. Over many years of coaching leaders through sabbaticals I have experienced four main types of sabbaticals.

It's important to reflect on where you've come from and what you've experienced in the last few years before you even plan your sabbatical. This helpful context will determine your needs during sabbatical. The rest you need as a parent of young kids may be the exact opposite of what you need as an empty nester. Take note that all four types can provide replenishment, but in very different ways.

The adventurous sabbatical. This is your chance to challenge yourself and experience unique environments. If life has felt humdrum or underwhelming and the routine is draining you then an adventurous sabbatical may be a great changeup.

One leader would zoom into our coaching sessions from their jungle bungalow in Costa Rica. He would tell me about the adventures of the week before, and the adventures of the upcoming week. A couple I was coaching would zoom in from their cliffside chalet in the Swiss Alps. They were hiking every day and exploring mountain villages. My warning about adventure sabbaticals is to not over-schedule them. Make sure to leave space, preferably at the end, to catch up, reflect on your adventures and prepare yourself to re-enter your work and routine. Buffer space is key here.

The reflective sabbatical. This is your chance to slow down, journal, rest and name what you've been through in the last season. If you've experienced transition, pain or weighty decisions this could be exactly what you need. If you picture times where no one needs you and you can tuck away with a book this is probably a sign you need a reflective sabbatical. This was the emphasis of one of my sabbaticals. I had been through lots of change and had published and promoted a book the year before. I decided to schedule this while my kids were in school to ensure lots of alone time. Although I'm an extrovert, I was craving time by myself where no one needed me. My times of journaling were rich, and time alone during the day allowed me to be very present with my family in the evenings. Even my adventures were relaxing, things like fly fishing, slow hikes and sitting in a mountain cabin by the fire. My warning about reflective sabbaticals is to make sure you have some things to look forward to. If every day is simply journaling and "normal things" you may not find a spark from sabbatical.

The connective sabbatical. This is your chance to dive deeply into relationships with family and friends. If you've experienced a busy work season or travel that has put space between you and your family this could be ideal. Many leaders with small kids choose a summer sabbatical where they can travel and make memories. Set proper expectations here. Travel with small kids is not designed for relaxation. Don't forget about time alone or time away with your spouse.

My warning about connective sabbaticals is to leave time for reflection. If you are making memories the whole time but have no space to process you will miss opportunities to learn about yourself and gain perspective. Most leaders underestimate the wear and tear of long trips. Many tell me afterwards that they wish they had traveled less and had more time at home as a family.

The hybrid sabbatical. Many sabbaticals are a combination of the other three. They involve some travel, some family time, some reflection space and some adventures. It's important to plan how the different aspects of your sabbatical will offer different opportunities and different challenges. Big trips can require lots of planning and yield jet lag. If you're staying home for most of your sabbatical you'll need more structure. Create a schedule your family can get used to. I highly recommend blocking off the mornings for reflection time and the afternoons and evenings for family time. This works well for many leaders. Then you can get time alone reflecting and plenty of family time without feeling like you are neglecting your family.

> What type of sabbatical do I need: adventurous, reflective, connective or hybrid?
>
> What factors in my life or leadership have created the need for this type of sabbatical?

Sabbatical "To-Don't List"

It's been helpful to many of my coaching clients to share this "To-Don't List" with them. You can share this with your organization, boss or team for clear expectations.

Don't...
- Skip preparation and coaching
- Avoid conversations with your spouse as you plan and prepare
- Expect a massive vision for your organization when you return
- Replace your work with other work (like writing a book or starting a side business)
- Over-schedule or under-schedule
- Compare your sabbatical to someone else's
- Isolate yourself
- Forget to look at your sabbatical plans or your Sabbatical Roadmap tool

Add any other sabbatical "To-Don'ts" below

-
-

The Sabbatical Journey

-
-
-
-
-

Get To's vs Have To's

"*Am I allowed to do this during sabbatical?*" I get this question a lot. First of all, it's not my choice. Secondly, it's helpful to walk through two simple categories together; *Get To's* and *Have To's*.

Get To's: Delights. Things you don't have to do but enjoy doing and people you enjoy being with.

Have To's: Duties. Obligatory things in your life or work and people you have to be around solely for work output.

You can't eliminate every *Have To* from your life during sabbatical, but you can eliminate most of them. Create as much space as possible to pursue *Get To's* during sabbatical. This simple question can be helpful, "Is the activity in question life giving, or is it life taking?" [33] It feels strange. Lean into the strange. This can be challenging, especially for those in ministry. I challenge everyone heading on sabbatical to pre-decide the activities you will and will not do and the people you will and will not be with. If work friends are *Get To* folks then get together with them, just let them know to steer clear of work. This helps to create clear boundaries and expectations, but it also limits the decisions you must make.

During one of my sabbaticals I had several friends struggling for different reasons. Instead of saying, "This stuff is heavy. They drain me right now." I realized I had an opportunity. Not only were they on my *Get To* list, but I had space to sit with my friends who desperately wanted to connect. I did not turn into a therapist or spend every waking moment with them, but I was able to be more of a supportive and caring friend than I would've been able to be if I was working. It was actually a joy to have the space to walk through their pain with them.

You may feel guilty about enjoying yourself while you're on sabbatical, especially if you work among the poor, your team is carrying a heavy load when you're away or your spouse cannot be on sabbatical with you. That's normal. Almost every leader feels a tinge of that. But experiencing delight is at the heart of sabbatical, and it's part of the replenishing process.

Create your Have To's and Get To's

Have To activities:

Get To activities:

Have To people:

Get To people:

Your Sabbatical Roadmap

It's important to sketch a pathway for your sabbatical ahead of time. In fact, this is exactly what you should be doing in the Prepare Phase. If you have a sabbatical coach, walk through this with them.

You will fill out the Prepare Phase and Experience Phase first. If you plan to experience international travel, you'll need to prepare for those blocks first. The length of your sabbatical will determine how you prepare in those months leading up to sabbatical. During the Experience Phase you will begin to get fresh dreams. This is when you can begin looking ahead and writing in the Reorient Phase.

SABBATICAL COACHING GROUP: *THE SABBATICAL ROADMAP*

PREPARE PHASE
preparation dates: _/_/_

List the tasks you must do in preparation for Sabbatical:

PERSONAL:

FAMILY:

WORK:

FAITH:

EXPERIENCE PHASE
sabbatical dates: _/_/_

List the things you would like to experience during Sabbatical:

PERSONAL:

FAMILY:

WORK:

FAITH:

REORIENT PHASE
return dates: _/_/_

Describe how you would like to be different when you return from Sabbatical:

PERSONAL:

FAMILY:

WORK:

FAITH:

DURING THIS SABBATICAL MY DEEP DESIRE IS TO:

© Sabbatical Coaching Group | Find more helpful tools at sabbaticalcoachinggroup.com

Your Sabbatical Structure

Now we're going to get a bit more detailed. Once you have your dates and boundaries in your Sabbatical Roadmap it's time to look at the calendar. It is VITAL to create a sabbatical structure well before your sabbatical– during the Prepare Phase. Without a structure to prepare for and things to look forward to leaders can dread sabbatical and even self-sabotage their sabbatical. It's okay to leave a few weeks open.

Week 1 *(Detox week)* **Dates:**

Focus:

Plans:

Location:

Week 2 Dates:

Focus:

Plans:

Location:

Week 3 Dates:

Focus:

Plans:

Location:

Week 4 Dates:

Focus:

Plans:

Location:

Week 5 Dates:

Focus:

Plans:

Location:

Week 6 Dates:

Focus:

Plans:

Location:

Week 7 Dates:

Focus:

Plans:

Location:

Week 8 Dates:

Focus:

Plans:

Location:

Week 9 Dates:
Focus:
Plans:
Location:

Week 10 Dates:
Focus:
Plans:
Location:

Reentry week **Dates:**
Focus:
Plans:
Warnings:

*Add more weeks below following the same structure if needed.

The Sabbatical Journey

Example: Alan's Sabbatical Structure

Instead of sharing a hypothetical example or talking about one of my clients, I'm going to show you my structure from my last six week sabbatical. I had a proactive posture, and I discerned that I needed a reflective sabbatical with some connection and adventure sprinkled in. My structure catered to my season of life, the ages of my kids, my wife's need to continue working full-time, my desires (like learning to weld) and a holiday week. You'll notice I only spent one week away from home, and I didn't even take any flights. The framework of detox, rest, reflect, relationships and prepare can be a helpful sabbatical structure.

> **Week 1** *(Detox week)* **Dates:** October 21-17
> Focus: Detox through being present and playing
> Plans: Rest with Julie, play in the mountains with friends
> Location: Mountain cabin
>
> **Week 2 Dates:** October 28-November 3
> Focus: Rest
> Plans: Lots of solo time, working out, reading and learning to weld
> Location: Home
>
> **Week 3 Dates:** November 4-10
> Focus: Reflection
> Plans: Look back at wins, clarify disappointments, welding
> Location: Home
>
> **Week 4 Dates:** November 11-17
> Focus: Relationships
> Plans: Life-giving lunches, calls with friends, hot springs day with friends, two fishing days, welding as time allows
> Location: Home and the mountains

Week 5 Dates: November 18-24
Focus: Prepare for the future
Plans: Dream sessions, meet with my coach, discuss future with Julie
Location: Home

Week 6 Dates: November 25-December 1 (Thanksgiving week)
Focus: Family time
Plans: Time with kids, Thanksgiving, cook, eat, relax, football, welding
Location: Home

Reentry week Dates: December 2-8
Focus: Reconnect with both of my teams
Plans: Listen to my team, journal each day, work out 3x, share my gleanings.
Notes: Enter slowly! My To Don'ts: Work more than 18 hours, schedule more work meetings, drill into small details or get through all emails!

The Sabbatical Thaw

After I had coached about fifteen leaders through sabbatical I saw a pattern emerging. I observed a progression where leaders would experience similar markers of replenishment along their sabbatical journey. I call this thawing out.

Jesus gives us the invitation: *"'Love the Lord your God with all your heart and with all your soul and with all your mind and with all your strength.' The second is this: 'Love your neighbor as yourself.'"* (Mark 12:30-31 NIV) Jesus describes five dimensions: heart, soul, mind, body and relationships. Many leaders experience thawing out in these five areas (and in this order).

The body usually thaws out first. Slowing down the body is essential. Labeling the first week as "detox week" is the best way to begin the natural process. I recommend scheduling very few activities and surrendering to sleep as much as possible. If you start with a huge movement toward spiritual activity and "finding God in every moment", you'll likely be disappointed. Submitting yourself to the process is key. Ruth Haley Barton reflects on a stressful season of life, family and ministry. She recalls, "I was too tired and worn out to find God - or anything else for that matter." [34] Sometimes the most spiritual thing we can do is sleep. Some leaders experience "the crash" (where they come down from adrenaline) while others report just being a little more tired than normal. Getting some walks or light hikes in can be helpful. One of the strengths of my sabbaticals has been outdoor exercise and even keeping (not increasing) my regular work out schedule at the gym.

This is where certain personality types will have to resist their motivations more than others. An Enneagram 1 may try to do everything perfectly by the book. An Enneagram 3 may try to crush sabbatical and take names! Those bent toward achievement will have to resist a lot here. Take note of what makes you feel uncomfortable in your first few weeks.

The mind usually thaws out next. It stops spinning, producing ideas and creating solutions. As leaders, this is what we've always done, and our minds have learned the patterns. But our minds need a break. Leadership survival has left us more worn than we think. Ruth Haley Barton says, "Our mind is tired of trying to hold it all together, figure everything out, make something happen..."[35] Let the mind rest. Don't read books that fire up the leadership lane in your brain. Instead read a novel, flip through a picture book (my personal favorites have cabins) or just take a break from reading until it feels like a *"Get To"* again. People often choose to read books during sabbatical on purposeful areas of life such as parenting, marriage or a topic that sounds intriguing. Follow your curiosity here.

The heart usually follows. Once the body feels rested and the mind has stopped spinning, the heart begins to bloom. This usually manifests in the leader feeling deeply present. People tell me how present they feel with God and others late into sabbatical. It's almost like they snap out of a trance. They can smell the freshness after a rainstorm, enjoy a sunset without reaching for their phone, savor a conversation without having to control it and cherish time with a friend. Many dads tell me they loved being so present to their families in the little moments: a walk to the park, ice cream on the back porch or enjoying Creation during a camping trip. These are usually the magic moments of sabbatical where leaders find themselves caught in the moment and full of wonder.

The soul almost always thaws out last. This means you're likely to experience a clearness and closeness to God toward the end of sabbatical. As I opened my journal about a week before my sabbatical concluded I wrote this phrase: "near and clear." That summed up my whole sabbatical; God was very near to me in the day-to-day activities and very clear with guidance and direction. When leaders desire to do something that feels very spiritual like a silent retreat or a field trip to a monastery I recommend it at least half way through sabbatical. That allows the leader to go through "the thaw out" and be more available to God. If they were to go the first few weeks of sabbatical they may be napping or spinning with thoughts about work.

Some pastors choose to tack a week or two of study leave on the end of their sabbatical. This can be a great choice. You're likely to be very calm and mentally sharp, and this can be a great space to put messages or teaching schedules together. (Later in this section I give some exercises that are helpful to capture and clarify sabbatical learnings while you're still thinking clearly but before you're back to work.)

Then we offer life through our relationships. When we have thawed out, replenished the things running low, reset our priorities and redesigned our schedule we return to our relationships with more to offer. We are in a better place to offer health and healing to those around us. Being away from our teams or congregations during sabbatical often makes the heart grow fonder. CEOs often miss the team meetings they hated, pastors can't wait to hug congregants and non-profit leaders feel reenergized to serve those who were beginning to drain them.

> Which dimension do I believe will need the most thawing out for me: body, mind, heart, soul or relationships?
>
> Why do I believe this is true?

The Awkward Process of Requesting a Sabbatical

I sat with Tim over a great cup of coffee. He is a phenomenal leader and a great guy, so I hoped I would get the opportunity to be his sabbatical coach. He told me about why he thought the next year was right for his first sabbatical, but he didn't know how to take steps toward it. Over the next ninety minutes I answered his questions, shared experiences of other leaders and talked through some of the tools in this field guide. He loosened up. I could see he was relieved, even a little excited. I let him know I would gladly share with his elder board to briefly educate them on sabbatical and ask them to support him in this desire.

A month later I shared some basics about sabbatical with the elders. I talked about the longevity it can cultivate, broken down the three phases and explained how Lead Pastors often return sharp and healthy. Then I asked him to exit the room. I bragged on his character and leadership capacity. Because the church was financially healthy I asked them to support him and his beautiful family so they didn't have to break their savings to get a nice vacation. They asked a few questions and began deliberating. After just a few minutes they had come to their decision: gift him the time off without responsibility, bless him well financially and resource him with a sabbatical coach.

He re-entered the room and they told him the news. A man who talks for thirty minutes publicly every Sunday could only squeeze out the words, "Wow! I don't know what to say!." I've had many experiences like this with elders, but this was my favorite.

How to Ask Your Board for a Sabbatical

If you desire a sabbatical but don't have permission yet here are some helpful places to start.

> I simply cannot recommend a driven, fast-paced, high-capacity leader receiving a sabbatical without a coach.

Educate the board or team. Most elders and board members don't come from a ministry background or a field where sabbaticals are common. They often want to support the pastor, but have underlying fears about how their absence will impact the church or organization. On most boards, a few members have no reservations and a few have fears about how the church or organization will fare when they're gone. They need the reassurance that, with coaching, they will develop a wise plan, work the plan and come back healthy and ready to go. Our team at Sabbatical Coaching Group has produced a short guide that helps boards understand what sabbatical is and isn't and answer their questions. I don't recommend having them read a whole book, as it may delay the process.

Get help advocating for your sabbatical. Get an advocate to share with your board or leadership team on your behalf. It's awkward to bring this up yourself, but a sabbatical coach or another pastor who has experienced a sabbatical can share with the board. This will likely put them at ease. We include this service in our sabbatical coaching process for no extra fee.

Pursue sabbatical coaching. After years of hearing sabbatical horror stories and investigating them deeper I saw two patterns. Sabbaticals gone wrong almost always had poor expectations or no ongoing guidance (coaching). Healthy sabbaticals almost always had a well-devised plan and ongoing guidance (coaching). For many years I've heard statements like, "Sabbatical saved my marriage," "I'm the kind of dad I always wanted to be," "I don't actually need to quit," and "I had no idea how exhausted I was." I simply cannot recommend a driven, fast-paced, high-capacity leader receiving a sabbatical without a coach. It is an investment, not an expense. A great sabbatical coach partners with God to care for and gently guide the leader through all three phases: the preparation for sabbatical, the experience of sabbatical and the reorientation after sabbatical.

> What is my next step with my board or team?

Clarifying Sabbatical With Your Organization

Once you have permission to receive your sabbatical it's vital to seek clarity with your leaders, supervisor or board before a sabbatical. The first person in an organization to pursue a sabbatical will likely have a lot of work to do. Clarifying beforehand will save a lot of headaches later. The purpose of a sabbatical is to renew a leader, but without clarifying the aim supervisors or boards may believe the leader should accomplish a big project during sabbatical. Before you begin planning your sabbatical, ensure alignment on the aim of sabbatical– and get this in writing. This will avoid confusion later. I'm a fan of no big projects on sabbatical. We're trying to depressurize the leader's environment, not stack them with more expectations.

If you are the first person in your organization to receive a sabbatical you'll be setting the tone.The first step is discussing sabbatical with your elder board in depth. Once you are aligned on the aim you can ask them to approve your time. Then you can discuss your sabbatical with your team. Use the following questions as anchors, and use your discernment when and with whom these fit best.

What is the purpose of a sabbatical season?

Why does our organization offer sabbatical?

What is the purpose of sabbatical in our organization?

What is sabbatical NOT for?

What resources will be allocated toward this sabbatical?

How long will the sabbatical be?

How did I settle on this timeframe?

Preparing Your Heart

Most leaders aren't prepared for the deep questions that arise during sabbatical. When work is no longer there to give us the dopamine hits, social interaction and tangible wins we ask deep questions. While this is part of the process, it's disorienting. We are so career-centric in our culture that we quickly define ourselves by what we do all week. Suddenly texts and emails cease and we sit in the quiet with big questions for ourselves and God.

During the Prepare Phase you're not just preparing your schedule–you're preparing your heart. It's easy to invest all of your energy in the trip plans, family schedule and the responsibility list for the team and neglect yourself. I hope this field guide gives you enough guidance to anticipate what you might experience during sabbatical.

> What specific things do I believe I will miss about my work tasks, environment or team?
>
> What emotions do I believe I will experience as I'm away from work?

The Sabbatical Journey

In what ways do I believe my work has become too central to my identity?

In what practical ways can I resist the pull to equate who I am with what I do?

Preparing Your Schedule

Scheduling wisely is vital to sabbatical. Most leaders who have a bad sabbatical experience waited too long to plan for sabbatical or didn't plan at all. Many leaders have told me, "I wish I would've planned better. My sabbatical would've been more enjoyable and fruitful." Some have told me they didn't have enough things to look forward to. Each day was like the last, and they felt wayward and purposeless. Those folks have told me, "Honestly, I was kind of bored." Others have over-scheduled. They say, "I wish my family and I would've had more time at home to just be". It can be very challenging to make big changes or fresh plans once sabbatical has begun. This is why the Prepare Phase is so vital.

What am I longing for most during sabbatical?

Describe what an under-planned sabbatical would look like for me ...

The Sabbatical Journey

Describe what an over-planned sabbatical would look like for me ...

What aspect of sabbatical do I need to plan for the most?

Preparing Your Family

One of the greatest opportunities sabbaticals offer is a chance to connect deeply with family. Those who are single often travel to see family or go on trips with their extended family. Those with kids in the house can be present and intentional with their kids without work getting in the way. Those who are empty nesters can enjoy times with their grown kids or grandkids. After getting on the same page as your spouse you should let your kids know what is coming. They will be excited. I encourage you to let them dream with you about what this time will hold. Get creative about the little things you want to do together, not just the big adventures.

Some parents co-plan small trips or fun activities with each kid, giving them a day or a few days to fully focus on them. After his sabbatical one dad told me, "I took my teenage kids to do things I never would've done. It allowed me to enter their world in a new way, and we'll never forget those experiences!" He had tears in his eyes as he told me this.

What opportunities does sabbatical offer to my family?

What opportunities does sabbatical offer to me as a parent?

What opportunities does sabbatical offer to my spouse?

What family challenges do I anticipate during sabbatical?

Co-Designing Your Sabbatical with Your Spouse

If you are married, it's vital that you and your spouse communicate clearly about sabbatical. Preparing for sabbatical with your spouse will help you avoid confusion and cultivate connection. I encourage you to journal through these questions first, have your spouse do the same and spend a few hours discussing your answers (ideally over a nice dinner).

What is my sabbatical for?

What isn't my sabbatical for?

What other types of work, if any, do I plan to do during sabbatical?

The Sabbatical Journey

What are my fears about sabbatical?

What are a few things I'm excited about for this time? Why?

What's on my "to don't list" for this time?

How do I think my spouse would answer these questions?

Time With AND Away From the Family

Many clients sheepishly ask me the question, "How do I.... you know... get the right amount of time away from my family?" It's actually a great question, and I bet you're asking it, too. Really what they're saying is, "I love my family and I want to be present with them and make lots of memories during this time, but I need to pull away to think and dream and hear from God. How can I do that without being a jerk to my kids or over-burdening my spouse?" That's better.

All parents feel this tension at some level, especially if they have little kids. Your first step when planning family time is to have an honest conversation with your spouse during the Prepare Phase. If you don't say anything and you both have different expectations, you're setting sabbatical up to create more tension than rest. This tension will produce disappointment, frustration and resentment for both of you. That's not what we're going for. Seek to determine what would be a great sabbatical for both you and your spouse.

The more travel a leader has during sabbatical the less structure they need. On the flip side, the longer periods of time you have with no "big plans" the more structure you should build in. Many leaders have followed a simple process that is clear and works for both sides: mornings are yours, the rest of the day is for the family.

Mornings are yours. This agreement allows you to wake up knowing you have a certain amount of time that's yours to control. You can sleep in, do something fun with a friend, sit at the coffee shop, hike, meander, read or intentionally hear from God. The time is yours. You have a definite end time that your kids and spouse can expect you home and expect you to be "on". The morning functions as an inhale and the rest of the day functions as an exhale.

The rest of the day is for the family. After filling your tank with a bit of sleep, connection with friends, solitude or adventure you come back to the family ready to invest. For summer sabbaticals this allows you to do afternoon adventures and enjoy the evenings together. This also allows your spouse to get time alone or take a break from the kids. Remember, you want this to be replenishing for both of you.

Others have created a variation of this liturgy that works for them. Some couples decide on designated free time for each of them on a different day of the week. Some have created daily rituals like family lunch, family dinner, a regular hour at the park or the after dinner walk. The main thing is making sure you have defined and agreed upon time boundaries that work for you, your spouse and the whole family. Some have even followed these rhythms while on vacations in pretty exotic places.

> What blocks of alone time are you hoping to get?
>
> What blocks of alone time could your spouse take advantage of?
>
> What family time can you agree on each day or week during sabbatical?

Preparing Your Mind

One of the biggest mistakes leaders make on sabbatical is stuffing their mind full of new concepts. They have a stack of books to "get through" during sabbatical. Sounds like homework. They are essentially trading their work tasks for a massive reading list. Avoid this temptation.

Do you have to ingest content as part of your job? If so, then strategic reading is work for you. I encourage you to rest from reading anything that directly applies to your field. If you are reading books or listening to podcasts related to your career field it will trigger your "work brain". You'll likely stir up work thoughts in that instant. I regularly read leadership, strategy, business and ministry books, so I have steer away from these genres during sabbatical.

I recommend you choose just one book that aims more at your heart and soul than your brain– and go through it very slowly. I often find that leaders struggle to read things that don't help them professionally. Guilty. Sabbatical is a time to read something just for the joy of it! The book you read on sabbatical should be a "get-to" not a "have-to" book. For you, maybe a "get-to" book is a biography, a fictional story or an old classic. Follow your curiosity. Perhaps it's time to pick up a book on parenting, marriage, one of your hobbies or a country you are visiting. This is not a time to pick up a book on how to grow your leadership, ministry or business

The Sabbatical Journey

Empty brain space is good for you, even though it will feel uncomfortable. New ideas, fresh vision and big dreams may sprout from this empty space. Don't fill it all up; give yourself space to just think.

> What topics should I stay away from during sabbatical? Why?
>
> What topics would I like to explore? Why?
>
> What book would nurture my heart or soul?

Preparing Your Team and Organization

It's vital to create clarity around sabbatical for your team and your organization. While it may seem obvious to you, you're going to need to tell them which areas you will be completely absent and unavailable. In relational organizations, especially in churches, there is a very fine line between work relationships and personal relationships. If you won't be getting together with the staff at all or attending the services on the weekend, let them know. If you won't be available for questions, let them know. It is far better to over-communicate here.

Sabbatical is perhaps the least talked about leadership development tool. When you are away, your team will be forced to stretch. Don't feel badly about this! A sabbatical is a great tool for growing your team's capacity. If you prepare them well, their capacity will grow as they step into new areas. If you prepared a team member well and they do not rise to the challenge while you're away they might not be a fit for the next season at your organization.

Sabbatical will give you a natural opportunity to delegate some of your tasks to someone else. If you recognize the need for delegation before sabbatical you can treat sabbatical as a "stress test" for your teammate. Prepare them to carry these tasks during your sabbatical by creating a specific task list. Go over this with them months before sabbatical and transfer these tasks to them a few weeks before sabbatical. When you come back to work you can gauge how well they carried these tasks during sabbatical and consider permanently transferring those to them after you return. This will give you space in your schedule and life to carry any new things God invites you to carry after sabbatical.

> What tasks or areas do I believe my team will miss me the most?
>
>
> Who is taking point on each of my tasks?
>
>
> When will I go over this task list with each team member?
>
>
> What tasks or areas would I like to hand over to someone else after my sabbatical?

Your Emergency List

Part of preparing your team for your sabbatical is clarifying what counts as an emergency. They should know ahead of time what they can take care of themselves, and when they should contact you. This is helpful for both sides. Your team will have a clear picture of what they are empowered to take care of in your absence. You will, in turn, be able to relax and enjoy your sabbatical knowing "no news is good news".

What specific things are emergencies I want to be contacted about? (this might include very specific numbers or circumstances like a budget dropping __% or a top tier staff member leaving)

> Who do I need to send this emergency list to?
>
>
> What specific things are emergencies I want to be contacted about? (this might include very specific numbers or circumstances)

Sabbatical Communication Plan

Many people carry secret baggage about sabbatical. When you under-communicate about sabbatical you're throwing kindling on sabbatical fears. You may lose trust and gain skepticism. Be proactive with your communication and celebrate the sabbatical as a feature of a healthy culture. For many, sabbatical is new and they don't know what it is or how to respond to it. Communicate early and often about sabbatical, especially if you are a visible leader in the organization. Here are a few principles about your sabbatical communication.

Private communication comes first. This involves sharing the why, what and when of your upcoming sabbatical with your team. I encourage you to do this with leaders one-on-one first and then share openly in staff meetings.

Public communication comes second. This is when you share with those outside the team, like clients, donors or the congregation. This should come after private communication. The team deserves to hear privately first before hearing this in a public setting. People will ask the staff for their opinion on your sabbatical, and they should be prepared with what they will say.

Timing is crucial. You don't want to communicate too far ahead, and you don't want to communicate last minute. I recommend mentioning this to your team six months out so they know it's coming and then begin actively preparing them for your to be away three months out. Four to six weeks out is usually sufficient for a congregational announcement. If you serve clients, plan as far out as they need to discern the changes. If you have a highly proactive culture you may need to back up your communication even further. Of course, use your discernment and your knowledge of the culture to create an appropriate communication schedule.

I recommend pastors make a big deal about sabbatical and make it visual in a few ways. This is especially true when it is the Lead Pastor, Executive Pastor or a highly visible leader. I highly recommend using video, because it can be said precisely once and utilized in multiple places. A high level leader can announce this or have an interview with the pastor who is leaving. This video can be shown in the service and sent via email. You don't want congregants to miss this and be surprised, even if they are out of town. I recommend gatekeepers praying over the leader, couple or family going on sabbatical during their last week as a public sending.

Your Private Communication Plan
Date(s):

Methods:

Next steps:

Your Public Communication Plan
Date(s):

Methods:

Next steps:

The Gentle Boat Ramp

Imagine sabbatical is a glassy lake, and your last month before sabbatical is a gentle boat ramp into that lake. The weeks before and after sabbatical carry inordinate weight, shaping your sabbatical and your next season of work. I encourage every client entering sabbatical to plan wisely for the month before sabbatical. This provides a far better entry into sabbatical. Try to avoid scheduling any big events or weighty meetings the last week before sabbatical. The goal is to enter sabbatical already moving down a gentle slope, not launching off a cliff. You can do the reverse as you reorient back into work after sabbatical. Every leader who has done this is grateful they did, without exception. After you've done all the above areas of preparation, here are some helpful timelines for the last weeks before sabbatical.

Three weeks before sabbatical. This will require a 100% capacity week. Do heavy lifting here. You will need to force your team to zoom out and look at the big picture of the next few months. Have very sharp one-on-one meetings with team members. Go over the schedule, task list and emergency list for your time away. Answer their questions, encourage them and clarify anything they need. You're trying to help them anticipate anything they'll need from you before you leave.

Two weeks before sabbatical. This should be a 75% capacity week for you. Imagine this is your last work week before you leave. Have your last one-on-ones with team members, going through their schedule

The Sabbatical Journey

and responsibilities while you're away.

The last week before sabbatical. This should be a 50% capacity week for you. You have answered questions from team members and direct reports. Ideally you are around half of the week being accessible and asking, *"Do you have any lingering questions for me?"* You basically want your team to say, *"Get out of here! Go ahead and be on sabbatical already."* That's a great sign that you've prepared them for your absence. Then you get to gently enter the Experience Phase of sabbatical.

> What are my next steps to make the ramp into sabbatical more gentle?

Relaxing into God's Presence

One reason for the gentle boat ramp into sabbatical is to begin the relaxation process before sabbatical officially begins. No, this isn't cheating. It's actually very wise and will allow you to get into the sabbatical flow sooner.

My friend, author and speaker Steve Cuss, uses this beautiful phrase that I've adopted: *relaxing into God's presence.* [36] It's a process, isn't it? God is always desiring a conversation but, like in human relationships, when we are rushed and distracted conversation doesn't just unfold. It can take some time to get there. Have you ever rushed into a date with your spouse? You're throwing on clothes, pulling your hair together (assuming you have hair), trying to pull up reservations on your phone and get a pizza thrown in the oven for the kids. Not exactly a recipe for deep, intimate conversation. It usually takes a few hours to relax into their presence. I have observed dozens of leaders relax into God's presence during sabbatical through "the thaw" process I described earlier. We can also learn to relax into God's presence on a daily or weekly basis. Many leaders cultivate a new rhythm for daily and weekly connection with God after their sabbatical.

For years I've relaxed my way into Sabbath. After a few years of a hectic ministry schedule I came to a glaring reality; *if I don't plan my week wisely it will continue planning me.* I was playing defense in my life, perpetually living a few minutes behind and it wasn't working for me. The stress was high and the quality of my life and work were low. So I intuitively created my first version of liturgy for my work week. In addition to blocking time to write sermons and other content, being with people and training leaders, I created a "Get To" work day each Thursday. My Sabbath was Friday, so I batched the most meaningful and energizing work tasks into my Thursday. It motivated me all week long to do the "Have To's" of work and ministry so I could enjoy the "Get To's" of ministry on Thursday. This literally changed my life. And my attitude. I began to relax my way into Sabbath instead of gritting my teeth and crashing into Sabbath. You are beginning the gentle descent into sabbatical. Resist the temptation to go fast, read too many books, lead yourself through sabbatical or grab for transformation. Trust the process and trust the Father.

PART THREE
The Experience Phase

The Experience Phase

Your sabbatical has finally begun! You have planned, prayed and prepared for this moment. It won't be all roses and butterflies, but there will be plenty of beautiful moments. I want to offer you a helpful grid to process your life and learning during sabbatical: *looking back, looking within* and *looking ahead*. No matter your profession, life stage or fatigue level this is a helpful grid to increase clarity and relieve the overwhelm.

Most leaders want to immediately dream about the future when their sabbatical begins. They may order a cappuccino and open a fresh page in their journal to scratch out their next big idea. It usually doesn't work that way. If you follow this general rule of thinking it will allow you to process the things you've been through the past few years, experience replenishment and eventually find some fresh perspective. I'm asking you to slow down, breathe– and let God guide you through sabbatical. Resist the temptation to lead yourself through sabbatical. I've watched this process create helpful guardrails for leaders as they create meaningful moments.

In this section, I'll warn you about disorienting emotions, arm you with exercises and walk you through progressions. Your experience will be unique, but you can learn from many others who have bravely forged the sabbatical journey before you.

The First Third: Looking Back

The first week of sabbatical can be quite a ride. The cocktail of excitement, fear, expectation and exhaustion can hit a leader hard. I encourage you to label your first week of sabbatical "Detox week". If you leave plenty of space during the first week you'll start to come down from the adrenaline you've been living off. Clearing the week to truly rest will likely feel strange for you. We're always more tired than we think, and this first week usually reveals that. Ideally you're not jumping on a plane, but if you have scheduled a trip to begin your sabbatical, your fatigue may be delayed. This week is a vital foundation for the rest of sabbatical.

I learned my favorite sabbatical analogy while getting my butt kicked on a reef off the coast of Kauai. A professional surfer took me under his wing, and offered to take me out for the day. It was a trial by fire situation. There was no warm up. We paddled way out to "first break", battling over waves until we lay flat on our boards awaiting "the big one". The only instructions he gave me were this: *"Watch me, and do what I do. When the wave takes you under don't fight it! Go limp; eventually you'll pop up."*

"Go limp?!?" I thought. My only real instructions were about falling, not surfing. I took beatings all day. I got chewed up and spit out by head high waves. I was sore for a week, but I did ride a massive wave– I'll never forget that moment!

If a wave of fatigue takes you under during sabbatical don't fight it; go limp. Eventually you'll pop out of the tiredness, and you'll feel better on the other side. If you don't, then you're not on the other side yet. Archibald Hart says, "When the post-adrenaline slump comes, the sooner you allow yourself to 'let down' the quicker your recovery will be. The more you fight it, the longer it will last."[38] These are basically withdrawal symptoms. Suddenly, the adrenaline that kept you producing during a normal week isn't needed. If you do experience a deep level of fatigue go with it. Take that nap. Sleep in. Put down that book. Just sit there for a while. I encourage you to leave your week one schedule very open. Your body needs to rest first before your mind can settle a bit.

> If a wave of fatigue takes you under during sabbatical don't fight it; go limp.

Some people also experience an emotional crash during sabbatical, even depression. I don't want to scare you, just prepare you. What's behind this crash? Sometimes the loss of adrenaline and the beginning of recovery naturally yields the blues or depression.[39] There are plenty of reasons for this from missing your coworkers to questioning your identity to having to deal with your disappointments eyeball to eyeball. During one of my sabbaticals I had one week where I hit the bottom emotionally. I engaged the painful thoughts, prayed through them, journaled about them and shared them with my wife. The next week, my buoyancy and optimism were back. The wave had spit me out.

On one of my sabbaticals I focused my "detox week" on connection and play. My wife and I savored our time next to the fire, in the hot tub, looking up at snowcapped peaks and walking through shops. Then I spent a few days with friends having fun in the mountains and resting. For me, zooming up mountain trails on an ATV, fly fishing in mountain lakes, eating great food and laughing was a great choice. This is what I needed, because these are activities that allow me to be fully present and forget the details of work. Be intentional about how you plan to detox and stick to the plan.

PART THREE | The Experience Phase

What do I need for my "detox week"?

What is my plan for this week?

The Fear of Pulling Away

*"A silent heart is a loving heart, and a loving heart is
a hospice to the world."* [40]
Catherine Doherty

The life of a leader is public. We live in glass houses with others peering in as we talk on stages, lead meetings and interact on social media. One of the deep challenges of leadership is facing failure and criticism in front of others. Eyes shift to us when we enter a room, and the tough decisions fall to us. The adulation, pushback and challenges come at us quickly. This can deform us as spiritual leaders. It's easy to live in fear of what others will do or how our actions will be perceived.

Distractions are everywhere! Email, social media, questions from the team and the task list will soak in whatever time we give them. It's hard to have a quiet conversation with God when we live in the subway station of leadership. While the pressure of the public eye has risen, it's not new. William Wilberforce, the abolitionist credited with abolishing slavery in Britain famously said, "I have been living far too public for me. The shortening of devotions starves the soul, it grows lean and faint. I have been keeping too late hours." Many of my leadership coaching and sabbatical coaching clients have told me: "It feels like everyone needs me all the time!" and "Everything matters too much to take a break." The issues leaders address are far too important to avoid breaks. Rest is an essential part of the life of a leader.

Bypassing rest can grind us down and erode our creativity. In the midst of incessant stress and public pressures many leaders fantasize about pulling away from it all. Deep down, we love the idea of people not needing us to lead them or make decisions for a bit. We also fear it. We know it's not about us, but we struggle to see how the organization can rotate without us. Fears blaze and questions consume us.

> Will we lose momentum on that big project during sabbatical?
> Will I lose followers if I jump off social media?
> Will I lose opportunities if my inbox is set to "out-of-office"?
> Will I lose credibility with my team if I don't see them for eight weeks?
> Will I lose the ability to push hard when I return to work?

> Many leaders heading on sabbatical realize they have secretly been addicted to attention, relevance and influence.

The fear of losing overtakes us when we pull away in our hyper-connected society. Below most of these is the fear of being anonymous. Putting away the laptop and putting on the sweatpants feels so good, yet so wrong. Many leaders heading on sabbatical realize they have secretly been addicted to attention, relevance and influence. If you're feeling this, you're not alone. Almost every leader I've coached through sabbatical finds it hard to imagine "the great disconnection" bearing fruit. After three sabbaticals I can tell you, it hasn't gone away, but it gets easier each time.

Jesus was no stranger to the pressure to produce. The crowds always wanted more: more preaching, more healing, more conversations after his life-altering spectacles. Yet he pulled away from the crowds to get time with his trusted team and his Father. And he only had three years of ministry time to live out his mission. How much more do we need to pull away than Jesus did? The demands of people, the necessity of tasks and the constant need to "feed the content beast" are tapping us on the shoulder. Our minds race thinking of everything we need to do in order to make our organizations spin. We need the next big donation to break ground on the building. We need to plan a year out on the schedule. We need to onboard the new staff member so they catch our DNA. The new campus is struggling and needs our oversight. And of course, Sunday is always coming for the pastor.

I've got good news; "Who you are is more important than what you do." While we desperately long to be loved and accepted for who we are this is a hard statement to accept. We've been trained not to believe it or receive it. Sabbatical forces us to enter the great unknown: a space where I will be known for who I am, not what I produce. We struggle to just "be." Perhaps we've never even experienced it. In fact, most leaders have done a little bit of everything except stepping away from work for long periods of time. Intentional rest may be our most underdeveloped leadership competency. Ruth Haley Barton asks an alarming question; *"Who am I when I'm not doing?"* [41] What a great question! Pay attention to yourself during sabbatical.

> What do you fear you will lose during sabbatical?
>
> How can you combat this fear?
>
> What is your reaction to the statement, "Who you are matters more than what you do"?

Weekly Sabbatical Check-In

I want to invite you into a helpful practice as you experience sabbatical. I encourage you to set a consistent time each week and check-in with yourself using the questions below. Transfer these simple questions into a journal and write two sentences or two pages.

Energy level (1-10):
Encouragement level (1-10):

What is good?

What is hard?

What is strange?

Where do I need to trust God?

My body. What am I experiencing in my body and my energy? What might be contributing to these things?

*My mind. What am I experiencing in my mind and my thoughts?
What might be contributing to these things?*

*My heart. What am I experiencing in my heart and my mood?
What might be contributing to these things?*

*My soul. What am I experiencing in my soul, my dreams and my connection to God?
What might be contributing to these things?*

*My relationships. What am I experiencing in my relationships and family?
What might be contributing to these things?*

Healthy steps for me this week:

Caffeine, Alcohol and Exercise During Sabbatical

You may want to reevaluate your beverage intake during sabbatical. I don't have an issue with alcohol or caffeine; I consume them both in moderation but stay on constant watch about them. They may work against what you are trying to accomplish during sabbatical. When we depend on them they can cause us to drift into bad cycles and resist God's natural rest process. Again, I am no sabbatical pharisee. I want the opposite for you: freedom and life to the fullest.

Reevaluating caffeine. Paired with adrenaline caffeine has a numbing presence in our lives. It can become a jolt to our system, and when relied on for a long time, can actually become an addiction. My caffeine intake had gotten a little out of control before my first sabbatical. In fact, I didn't drink coffee until we adopted two kids and then, well, it became a "very important habit" to my day. I wondered how it was impacting me, so I planned to test this by going off it cold turkey when my sabbatical began. As you can imagine, I felt a massive crash when I stopped the meetings, the output and the coffee consumption all at once. I got my answer.

Sabbatical can be a great time to experiment with less caffeine. You may be surprised that you no longer need it once you get adequate sleep and regulate your adrenaline. Caffeine interrupts the body's natural healing and rest processes. Reevaluating this can bring some health and even freedom.

Reevaluating alcohol. You can apply the same thinking to alcohol on sabbatical. Like caffeine, it can actually work against the rest and replenishment you're seeking. There's plenty of research on how alcohol disrupts sleep and replenishment cycles. Of course, covering tough emotions with alcohol can enable us to avoid the very things we should be thinking about in order to get healthy. Sabbatical is a good time to step back and make sure you don't have an issue with alcohol. Some folks decide to take time away from it for a time during sabbatical. Others enjoy having more space in their schedule for a drink and a long conversations with a friend or their spouse on the porch. The lack of structure and work could lend itself to unhealthy habits with alcohol. At the end of the day, sabbatical provides an opportunity for both wisdom and freedom.

Reevaluating exercise. You might find it strange that I batch exercise with what some may consider vices. Hear me out. Exercise is an incredible tool and gift in itself, but a terrible master. Plenty of people have perverted views of exercise that warp how they rest or do not rest. My wife, Julie, reminds me that I don't need to earn time sitting on the couch with exercise.

Everyone has a different take on exercise during sabbatical. Some choose to upscale exercise. Perhaps they are experiencing physical issues, have new health goals or exercise has gotten crowded out of their weekly schedule. Some leaders exercise too much during sabbatical due to boredom. One leader I coached failed to work his plan, and he confessed he went to the gym for multiple hours a day. He didn't know what else to do. Others choose to downshift their exercise. Maybe they've been training hard for something and want to pull back. Many people discover the joy of walking daily during sabbatical. Wherever you stand with exercise during your sabbatical try to not make it a chore or another thing to strive for or measure.

Here's my invitation: find the kind of exercise that fits your sabbatical desires. Maybe it's even fun for you. Get outside into Creation as much as possible. Sunshine, movement and vitamin D is a game changer! During my last sabbatical I chose to keep the same exercise schedule at the gym and create space for hiking and running. This was both healthy and effective for me in light of my goals.

> What wise changeup can I make with caffeine and alcohol during sabbatical?
>
> What will my approach to exercise be during sabbatical?

The Fruitfulness of Extended Time Away

Solitude does work in us, and eventually does work through us. Solitude may be a place of wilderness for you; a space that feels scary and unknown. Solitude may force you to pay attention to thoughts you'd rather ignore. It feels easier to stay busy and keep the ear buds in. But here, in the wilderness of solitude, God begins to speak, comfort, challenge and heal.

Henri Nouwen called solitude, *"the furnace of transformation."* [42] Furnaces get hot and burn things up. They also heat a home, fire a clay pot or cook a delightful pizza. Through the fire, and sometimes pain, of being alone God meets us. Don't rush past what God is burning in the fire to get to what God is producing through the fire. Sabbatical solitude is for listening, not producing. I invite you to receive during your solitude. Read the book that sparks your interest. Journal about the good, hard and disorienting thoughts. Don't write long sermons, spend a week on your next business plan or start on your next book. Be patient and work the process. And let God do work in you through the process.

The Apostles Paul and John both had extended time in solitude. It shaped and formed them first in the fire. It's clear from their writing they had a fire in their bellies. This time and space allowed them to think deeply. In his quest to spread the gospel and equip church leaders Paul regularly had long boat rides. These days and weeks of doing "nothing" but thinking, praying and writing bore a lot of fruit. He also wrote some of his best stuff while in prison and on house arrest. The Apostle John was on the rocky island of Patmos thinking, praying and writing. They were transformed in solitude. When you read their writing you can feel it. It's jarring. It's intense. It's transcendent. I wonder of much of the New Testament would have been written without these forced stations of solitude?

What scares me about solitude?

Why do I need solitude during sabbatical?

When will I regularly schedule solitude into my sabbatical schedule?

Assessing Your Tiredness

This is a great exercise to do during your sabbatical to help you uncover what may be at the root of your fatigue. You have the time and space to zoom out, get a wide angle lens of your life and reverse the cycle you've been living in.

Step 1: Assess the Level of Your Tiredness

Not all tiredness is created equal. As a coach, I want to understand the level of tiredness the leader is experiencing.

Expected fatigue. You've been running hard for a relatively short time (six months or less), and this fatigue was expected. You have a timeline and an actual plan to slow down. As long as you have a true time of rest coming (your sabbatical) and a shift to your routines replenishment is on the way.

Extended fatigue. You've been running hard for an extended time (more than six months), and you have no plan to reverse this. It may be mysterious to you. You may wonder, "Why am I SO tired?" This is dangerous, especially if you have no plan to slow down or a plan to replenish. Sabbatical is an ideal time to develop a reversal plan.

Extreme fatigue. In this zone you're heading toward burnout. You've lost desire to do a lot of the things you love (ironically those things can help you replenish), and you've accepted the reality of your fatigue as normal for far too long. You may have real and pressing reasons for this like young children or family medical issues. You don't know how to reverse this and you're not sure you have the energy. You are experiencing numbness in many areas, and you could be experiencing depression, also.

If you are in extended fatigue or extreme fatigue, I recommend going to the doctor to get bloodwork done. There may be an underlying medical issue. I also recommend good therapy to identify the root causes of your overwork or over-extension.

What is my level of tiredness: expected fatigue, extended fatigue or extreme fatigue?

Step 2: Assess the Source of Your Tiredness

In order to make changes you'll need to evaluate which aspect of your life is most tiring. Don't just think about work and home, it's more nuanced than that. Here is a helpful grid.

Body. Your physical body is worn down. Common causes can be lack of sleep, lack of exercise, bad eating habits or a lack of margin.

Mind. Your mind is overextended. Common causes can be screen habits, working in the evenings, leading in too many areas, work that tilts away from your unique design, too many decisions, and pervasive change.

Relationships. Your relationships are a source of constant stress and conflict. Common causes can be people who take from you but don't give back, ongoing low-grade conflict or family drama.

Heart. You have experienced significant loss and may not have had space or a process to grieve it. Common causes can be major changes personally or professionally, painful incidents you haven't dealt with or hopelessness in a certain area.

Soul. You have had tectonic shifts in your identity, faith or family. Common causes can be lack of purpose, a faith crisis or the loss of a job that was connected to your identity. It's often a combination of these areas, but try to pinpoint one area that hurts the most.

Which area of my life is the greatest source of tiredness right now; body, mind, relationships, heart or soul?

Why?

Step 3: Make Changes to Reverse the Cycle

Regardless of your tiredness level, you must take action. The moment we're "sick and tired of being sick and tired" is a key moment to create a plan to reverse the cycle. Habits you create in the ReOrient Phase after your sabbatical can solidify new patterns and energy levels.

We've undervalued and under-understood the power of rest. Rest is not just getting your sweatpants on and sitting on the couch. You may want to learn more about the seven types of rest from Physician Saundra Dalton-Smith to see which ones you are lacking. [43] Each type of rest can bring replenishment to a particular flavor of strain. Our narrow view of rest limits our replenishment. We've skipped over certain things that we don't think "count" as rest that could actually replenish us deeply. The flavor of your fatigue should shape the flavor of your rest.

If the currency of leadership is energy, not time, we must evaluate our energy carefully. Each person is unique. In order to reverse our energy drains we must be aware of them. We must also know what fills us.

Drains. These are things that take energy from us. They go against the grain of who we are. While we can't avoid all of these in our home and work, we can be aware of them and limit them. Your *"Drains List"* should cover personal and professional items.

Fills. These are things that lift your energy and your spirit. These big or small things enliven you and get you going. Your *"Fills List"* should also cover personal and professional items. Once you are aware of them you can practice them regularly. Be as specific as possible.

MY DRAINS	MY FILLS

Once you identify the level and source of your tiredness and acknowledge your drains and fills, you can create a plan for what you will START doing, STOP doing and KEEP doing to reverse the tiredness cycle. I modified a popular tool called "Start, Stop, Keep." It can be very effective in creating a reversal plan for your exhaustion. Just filling this tool in won't change your life; you have to act on the life and leadership commitments every week. I challenge you to utilize sabbatical as a experiment with many of these.

SABBATICAL COACHING GROUP: *START, STOP and KEEP*

STOP DOING: *What is eroding my health and impact that I need to stop doing immediately?*

1. _____ WHY: _____
2. _____ WHY: _____
3. _____ WHY: _____

START DOING: *What can I start doing immediately to increase health and impact?*

1. _____ WHY: _____
2. _____ WHY: _____
3. _____ WHY: _____

KEEP DOING: *What is producing fruit that I should continue doing?*

1. _____ WHY: _____
2. _____ WHY: _____
3. _____ WHY: _____

DESIRE TO STOP DOING: *What do I desire to stop doing eventually that is currently necessary?*

1. _____ WHEN: _____
2. _____ WHEN: _____
3. _____ WHEN: _____

DESIRE TO START DOING: *What do I desire to start doing eventually that is currently unrealistic?*

1. _____ WHEN: _____
2. _____ WHEN: _____
3. _____ WHEN: _____

© Sabbatical Coaching Group | Find more helpful tools at sabbaticalcoachinggroup.com

What do I need to START, STOP and KEEP doing?

When will I quit or repeat each of these?

Step 4: Cultivate a Regular Replenishment Cycle
We started by gaining awareness of the level and source of your tiredness. Then you made commitments to remove the things that drain your energy and repeat the things that give you energy. But in order to create ongoing replenishment you must create habits that help you replenish regularly. An annual vacation is not enough to sustain the rigors of navigating our culture, caring for our family and doing meaningful work week after week.

Energy leaks effortlessly, but replenishment requires intentionality. If you don't calendar your replenishing activities and turn them into habits, urgent matters will eat them up. When habits slip it's easy to slide back into a tiredness cycle. Habits are ten dollar investments that give ten thousand dollar returns. You may experience small gains quickly from your habits, but expect sixty days of practicing your new habits before you see any serious lift. That's how investing works.

Here are a few guideposts for creating replenishing habits.

Plan for the long haul. As Stephen Covey says; *"Begin with the end in mind."* [44] As you plan your habits think about what you can sustain for an extended period of time.

Focus small. Habits compound. When you take small steps you prove to yourself you have what it takes. Keep collecting small wins like compounding interest.

Repeat them regularly. When you know the steps you're going to take put them on your calendar, as if they're a vital meeting or task, because they are. The more often you repeat these replenishing habits the more energy you'll get. Make them automatic and easy to repeat.

Momentum and routine are your friend. Capitalize on the momentum of small wins, and seek to transfer that to other areas.

Raise your commitment as you go. When it comes to growth I'm a fan of evolution, not revolution. As you stack your wins you can increase them slowly as you and your schedule are ready. Starting with huge commitments can lead to discouragement and quitting, like most New Years resolutions. [45]

Wins and Disappointments

Exhaustion causes us to lose our perspective. We can lose vision amidst our fatigue and busyness. It's important to name the victories you've experienced early in sabbatical or you lose sight of how far you've come and how God has provided for you. These wins can range from beautiful moments to big epiphanies. On my sabbatical I found myself extremely grateful for a major milestone I crossed, two close friends who supported me and my growing relationship with one of my children.

I did the following exercise in a coffee shop. It was awful and freeing to write down my disappointments. Clarifying these things produced a temporary sadness. I recognized that some areas of my life were not as I hoped they could be or should be. But it was fruitful. In fact, it was the hinge moment of my sabbatical, a turning point. I had hit the bottom of the pool, and, even though I was twelve feet under, feeling pressure on my ears, I could spring up to the surface for air.

Celebrating Wins

Leaders are notoriously poor at celebrating wins. We tend to over-index on vision, goals and strategy and forget to celebrate progress. The following exercise will help you name the big and small wins you've experienced.

The Sabbatical Journey

I am grateful for the following wins in my life...

Naming Disappointments

Disappointment centers around unmet expectations. During sabbatical there is very little to distract a leader and very little to hide behind. Every human carries gnawing disappointments, although we are

PART THREE | The Experience Phase

rarely aware of them. Early in your sabbatical it's helpful to name the disappointments you have experienced over the last few years. Some people choose to zoom out and examine the last decade.

Family
What I hoped for…

What I got…

Finances
What I hoped for…

What I got…

Health
What I hoped for…

What I got…

Work
What I hoped for...

What I got...

Relationships
What I hoped for...

What I got...

Other area:
What I hoped for...

What I got...

The Second Third: Looking Within

I wish someone had prepared me for the disorientation of my first sabbatical. I didn't have a framework for sabbatical or a progression to work through. As you move past the first third of your sabbatical get ready to process new things. Hopefully your body is resting and your mind is clearing. Here are some things many leaders experience during sabbatical.

Disorientation. This is the number one word I discuss with leaders during sabbatical coaching sessions. Sabbatical is disorienting for so many reasons. Your life, your schedule and your routine are nearly unrecognizable. It is strange to wake up without a professional checklist. Suddenly life opens up. You have space to examine new things and reexamine old things. With our work out of the way we become more aware of our other roles.

What aspect of sabbatical is most disorienting? Why?

Gratitude. You may catch yourself blown away by the opportunity to take extended time away from work. When you experience one of these moments say a short prayer or text someone who made this sabbatical possible. This is one of the greatest gifts you can ever be given!

What aspect of sabbatical am I most grateful for?

Who can I reach out to and thank?

Lightness. Leaders often tell me how light sabbatical feels. It's strange to not carry the weight of decisions, the load of emails and the pressure of major projects.

In which areas am I feeling the lightness of sabbatical?

Space. Part of the disorientation is having so much space in your schedule and your brain. You don't have to squeeze time with God, friends or family into the cracks of your life during sabbatical– it's the main thing. It's vital to have just enough structure for your days so you don't wake up with no clue what to do that day. Know your tendencies. If you tend to over-commit your time, leave plenty of space. If you tend to waste time, schedule a few meaningful activities.

What is the best use of my extra space during sabbatical?

How am I different when I have space?

Lack of production. Not producing at work is a double-edged sword. On one hand it can feel delightful not to be responsible for everything you normally would be. On the other hand the loss of dopamine hits from completed tasks can make a leader feel empty. This lack of production can feel, you guessed it: disorienting.

What is great about not producing professionally during sabbatical?

What is hard about not producing professionally during sabbatical?

Loss of pressure and overwhelm. Many leaders are stepping out of overwhelm into sabbatical. There is usually a depressurization that takes place progressively throughout sabbatical. It takes some time to move from pressure to relaxation, so leave plenty of space for this. This loss of pressure can help leaders feel clear-headed and full of vision, but can also leave them asking, *"Am I going to be able to get back on the work train and ride it?"*

> The busyness and complexity of our lives often drowns out God's whispers.

In which areas am I feeling this loss of pressure?

How am I different without this pressure?

The nearness of God. I'm glad to say many leaders sense the closeness of God as a friend during sabbatical. I'm not guaranteeing you'll hear God speak, but it often happens naturally. The busyness and complexity of our lives often drowns out God's whispers. When we're listening for God we often hear Him.

In what ways have you sensed the nearness of God during sabbatical?

In what environments do I most often sense God's nearness?

Disappointment or sadness. We resist sabbath, solitude and silence, in part, because we will have to deal with things we would rather avoid. This has been true during all three of my sabbaticals. My "disappointments list" is both the most painful thing and most fruitful thing I did. Once I had clearly named them I could embrace the sadness of the disappointments, pray through them, discuss them with my wife and friends and move forward. The good news is when we sit with our sadness and disappointment we can begin to deal with things. They are now in the light.

What areas am I most sad about?

Why?

What disappointment is most painful?

Why?

Deep relational presence. Leaders often tell me how they loved being fully present with family and friends during sabbatical. Their phone and laptop disappeared, and they received the gift of deep presence. They felt closer to their spouse and kids. They were able to savor the moments and the simple things.

In what ways do I feel closer to others or God right now?

In what areas do I feel distance between me and others or me and God?

Getting spun up. I was a few weeks from going back to work. I was well-rested with fresh perspective. I even looked relaxed, reclining a bit, legs crossed in my favorite chair with a book in hand. My wife, Julie, walked in the room with one statement that instantly changed my demeanor; *"We need to make a decision on our healthcare plan."* She didn't mean to spoil my relaxing afternoon, but I spun up immediately. I instantly thought of the thousands it would cost us and the hours I would waste scanning websites. Clearly I wasn't as resilient and at peace as I thought I was. I took some deep breaths, and marked off a few hours to take care of it a few days later. It spoiled my afternoon, but not my sabbatical or even my week.

No matter how well you prepare for and work the plan for your sabbatical you will get spun up a few times. These moments will come during and after sabbatical. You won't be immune to them, but perhaps they won't hit as deep or last as long.

What moments or experiences spin me up or stress me out?

Why do I spin up during these times?

What lies do I believe in these moments?

Finding a Hobby

> *"In God's economy, to redeem time,
> you might just have to waste some."* [46]
> Mark Buchanan

I was waist deep in freezing cold water laughing out loud. Every fly I casted looked like food to the rainbow trout that day. I walked back to my car grinning ear to ear from one of the best fishing days of my life. Sometimes I catch fish out there, sometimes I get my best ideas, and sometimes I just have fun. I don't think I'll ever become a professional fly fishing guide. I don't really want to.

I can't drive to a high mountain lake every week, so I pick up a design magazine next to the blazing wood stove or build something in my garage. I love doing light design projects, but I'll probably never be a professional designer. I just love sketching up a project and figuring out how to pull it off.

Hobbies can feel like a waste, but they're one of the best investments we can make. Hobbies fall into Stephen Covey's "important, but not urgent"[47] category. Hobbies remind us we care about other things than our job, and can help us take our minds off our work. A hobby is a non-essential activity you regularly practice simply for enjoyment. Many things should stay in the "simply for enjoyment" category. I knew a guy who turned his fly fishing hobby into a goal of catching

The Sabbatical Journey

100 fish that year (yep, he's an Enneagram 3). I took some guys fishing, and he was deeply bothered that the fish weren't biting that day. We called it a day to enjoy a cold beer and a fine cigar on the bank. Hobbies can provide the following:

> Mental rest away from work
> Fun
> Energy replenishment
> Distraction from weighty issues
> Renewed passion for our family
> Creative reset
> Solutions for problems we're trying to solve

Hobbies can bring lightness and buoyancy back to our lives. Try combining your needs and passions like exercise, outdoors, fun and social connection. It might be time to accept the invite to the biking club, frequent trivia night, plan the fishing excursion or join the book club you've been thinking about just for the enjoyment of it.

It's easy to fall out of touch with hobbies. The weight of responsibility at work and at home can push hobbies aside. When we feel maxed out at work and at home, and when money is tight, hobbies are the easiest thing to cut. But if you ignore them you're missing out on joy and replenishment. Don't be fooled; hobbies are way too important to ignore. [48]

Sabbatical is an ideal time to discover or rediscover hobbies. Sometimes people begin to get a little bit bored during the middle of their sabbatical. That's okay. Perhaps this is an ideal time to experiment with a hobby. Try something out that you've also wanted to. Work on your golf swing, take the pottery class, build the bookcase you've been thinking about, get back into baking or pull out your fishing rod.

> What hobby can I experiment with during sabbatical?

> What hobby would I like to continue after sabbatical?

Zooming Out

I want to invite you to consider a profound question; *"What is the good life for you and your family?"* Not a decent life. Not a life others view as successful. A good life that is meaningful, fulfilling and aligns with what matters to you. A life like this, of course, is much bigger than our work. We can't cheat off someone else's paper here. The answer to this question is different for all of us, and it will determine our route up the ridges of the peaks we endeavor to climb.

Jesus was a master question asker. When a man came to him for healing he asked a surprising and disarming question; *"What do you want me to do for you?"* He wanted to know what they wanted before he helped them, even if it seemed obvious. Isn't this what a great friend, coach or partner does? Asks questions about what we want without assuming.

Before working on goals with leaders I start by asking them to paint a picture of the good life. Their values, dreams and desires naturally leak out during this process. One leader may want to be a great parent while another has a revenue goal that would lift the quality of life for their family or employees and another has the goal of retiring early and working in a non-profit. Others want a lifestyle of travel, time off work, adventure or flexibility to care for their aging family members. Our vision of "the good life" will determine the peaks we endeavor to climb, and the ones we don't. Leaders of depth think more about their eulogy than their year end reports. Pause to paint a picture of the good life a decade from now. [49]

What is "the good life" for me and my family three years from now? Describe this in as much detail as possible…

What is "the good life" for me and my family ten years from now?

Impact Goals and Identity Goals

The topic of goals is polarizing among leaders. Some leaders get excited as they head into goal planning season, others have sworn off formal goal setting. Some have a goal setting process that works well for them, but most haven't found that yet (but probably won't admit it). That was me for years. Here are some of the cracks in our traditional goal setting process.

We focus too much on visible professional goals and too little on invisible character goals. What good is it to hit our professional goals if our family is falling apart, our heart is empty, our body is wasting away and we're burning out?

We clarify our goals, but we don't clarify what we will invest to meet them. How can we set proper goals if we don't know the tradeoffs we're making?

We don't have a pathway to meet our goals, so they only remain as dreams. What steps will I regularly take to reach these goals?

In light of these three cracks I worked to create a process for setting goals that synthesized two things: goals focused on who we are becoming below the surface and goals focused on what we do above the surface. Both matter, but we must connect them.

Every investment is based on delayed gratification; if we do small things along the way we will have more later. Anything you truly want is worth investing in. I've found investment language to be helpful when talking about goals.

Who I want to become; invisible roots. These are the things that are deep, relational, intimate, long-lasting and largely invisible.

Some examples: Relational connection with family and friends, culture goals, spiritual practices or health goals.

What I want to do; visible fruits. These are the things that can be easily counted and likely get celebrated by others.

Some examples: Revenue goals, new projects, organizational goals or a home purchase.

Invest about an hour on the Growth Game Plan on the next page. The leaders who invest in this process reference it years later. [50]

SABBATICAL COACHING GROUP: *GROWTH GAME PLAN*
A process to identify and invest in your dreams:

DREAM:
INVESTMENTS

DREAM:
INVESTMENTS

DREAM:
INVESTMENTS

DREAM:
INVESTMENTS

DREAM:
INVESTMENTS

DREAM:
INVESTMENTS

IMPACT DREAMS — What I want to do; visible fruits
IDENTITY DREAMS — Who I want to become; invisible roots

© Sabbatical Coaching Group | Find more helpful tools at sabbaticalcoachinggroup.com

The Last Third: Looking Ahead

This is the home stretch of your sabbatical. During this time you will likely experience a few counterbalancing things.

You will be thinking clearly about life and priorities. You are likely feeling rested and more clear about your priorities after time away from work. But this clarity can be scary as you see the sabbatical finish line approaching.

Your head will start to naturally spin up for work again. Your brain knows you're going back. Some people experience this as excitement, others as anxiety, most as a combination of the two.

You will begin to think about necessary changes. You'll naturally scan your life and leadership and evaluate necessary changes. These will be both exciting and scary. You'll experience some doubt on whether you have the ability or freedom to change these areas. You may be tempted to villainize work for the things it gets in the way of.

During the last few weeks of sabbatical you should begin anticipating your return. If you do not plan it I promise; it WILL plan you. Sabbatical can feel like a dream world devoid of responsibility and stress. Leaders naturally redesign their lives on sabbatical as they dream ahead. But they are doing this without many of the details, stressors and expectations that will soon hit them. While we can't predict the future it's very valuable to anticipate what might await you as you return. In addition to your commitments, this anticipation process can be very helpful as you experience these things.

My Journal Entry: "Time to Return"
Today is my 43rd day in a row not working. I head back in just a few days and the emotions are swirling. Here's what I'm feeling as I prepare to return.

I feel clear. I am thinking very clearly. Fewer things have been competing for my attention, and the ones that have, deeply matter to me. Fresh dreams and clear realizations are at the front of my mind. I remember what matters.

I feel present. I have felt very present to God and my family during most of this time. I've been able to be with my kids, sit at their events and at meals not mulling over the day. As Julie and I talk at the end of the day I'm not struggling for brain space to listen or the energy to stay locked into the conversation. God spoke to me through journaling, walks and good coffee sessions. The space was beautiful!

I feel afraid. I don't want to lose how I've grown. I'm afraid the freshness will just fade away and I will make decisions that compromise my new commitments.

I feel grateful. Above all, I'm full of gratitude for God's love, not conditional on anything I do or don't do. I'm grateful for the support I received to be able to take this cosmic pause. The timing was perfect, and the planning was on point. No regrets. I'm fully aware these thoughts and decisions will mark me for a long time. These weeks will impact years, maybe decades.

Telling Others About Your Sabbatical

People will ask a dreaded question when you return from sabbatical; *"How was it?"* This is akin to going on a year long adventure in the jungles of Peru and living among native tribes. A friend asks, *"How was it?"* It's hard to know what to say. What complicates it even more is the depth of learning. Most people aren't ready to hear about the condition of your soul in the line at Starbucks.

Life will soon gain speed and complexity. While you are still thinking clearly it's time to get some thoughts on paper. Writing things down will help some of the anxiety dissipate. Some of these things are for your eyes only, others will be helpful to read to your spouse or close friend. You may share a few of these thoughts with your team or friends who ask about your time. Don't edit as you write, just get your thoughts on paper in these last few weeks of sabbatical.

How I Experienced the 6 R's of Sabbatical
Make a brief list of how you experienced these areas from your sabbatical preparation process.

> Recreation: How I experienced moments of fun, enjoyment or creating.

Rest: How I experienced replenishment in body, mind, heart and soul.

Reconnection: How I reconnected with God.

Relocation: What new places I experienced (even if they were local).

Relationships: How I invested in friends or family.

Resources: How finances or relationships were a gift during sabbatical.

Translating your experience and growth to others is a big challenge. Before you head back to work think through what you'll share with friends and coworkers. It's helpful to create the five minute version you can lace into a conversation, the fifteen minute version you can share with your team and the sixty minute version that you can share with an interested friend over lunch.

Church settings are unique. If you're a pastor the staff and congregation will both want to hear about it, but they need something slightly different. People don't need to know everything you did; they want to hear what you learned and how you grew. Some of your staff are actually scared that you have a huge vision that they need to implement. Instead, they may need to hear simple things like, *"I realized how much I love being a Dad"*, *"I realized I love my work here"* or *"I need to take Sabbath more seriously every week."* Resist the urge to think you need to share some huge lesson from your sabbatical. You're also painting accidental expectations for those who experience sabbatical after you. The following exercise can help you solidify what you learned during sabbatical.

My Top 10 Sabbatical Learnings List

You have learned a lot during sabbatical. This list is helpful for the sake of processing your learning and for the sake of sharing your learnings with others. It can help you as a cue sheet to share parts of this list with your team or your congregation.

Here are a few of my Top 10 from one of my sabbaticals…

- *Clear thinking requires space. I need more space in my daily and weekly schedule to simply think, reflect, play and create. It makes me less anxious, more grounded and more present with friends and family. This is also where many of my greatest contributions to leaders are formed.*
- *What got our organization here will not get us there. I can celebrate the things that got me and us to this point, but I must eliminate some things if we are going to mature and serve leaders at the level we need to.*
- *Pulling away from my commitments has been helpful to reevaluate my life. Near-sightedness blinds us. It's helpful to empty "the junk drawer" to see what should be put back into my schedule.*
- *Working with my hands grounds me. With so much intangible brain work every week I need tangible handiwork. I need to make physical things.*

The Top 10 things I learned (or re-learned) During Sabbatical

-
-
-
-
-
-
-
-
-
-

Post-Sabbatical Commitments

Most people experience a surprising, even scary, level of clarity during sabbatical. Perhaps the greatest challenge of sabbatical is translating the things you learned on sabbatical into lasting change. Wise leaders translate what they learned during sabbatical into commitments after sabbatical. Change unfolds when we translate new awareness into new actions. Once we have clarity we must take courage. This is where sabbatical coaching shines: helping you name how you want to be different after sabbatical and helping you commit to new actions. These new actions will carve new pathways into your life over time. I experienced this after my last sabbatical.

The greatest gift from my sabbatical was space to think, relax and just be. I realized I needed to leave one whole day open from coaching in the middle of each week. This would allow me to stay grounded and continue creating valuable resources for leaders. This was a scary thought as I added up how much a commitment to cut one day of coaching might cost our business. After assessing the risk I realized it was worth whatever it would cost. After looking over my calendar I realized Tuesdays would be the ideal day. I scratched out a new big picture schedule for my return. A few days later I tightened it up a bit and sent it over to my team to help me solidify before I returned to work. There was no turning back.

The Sabbatical Journey

I am writing these words on a Tuesday. With some work, and the help of my team, I figured out how to work around these days. Tuesdays have become an anchor for me. They've also provided the space I need to create meaningful resources, like this field guide. One of my teammates has also started blocking off time on Tuesdays to write.

In the last few weeks of sabbatical it's vital to create a list of commitments you will make in life moving forward. Many of these are based on your Top 10 Learnings List. Here are a few of my commitments I penned about a week before I returned to work:

- *Recommit to two dates a month with Julie.*
- *Block off Tuesdays for thinking and writing.*
- *Create something tangible with my hands every week.*

Now it's your turn.

Here are some commitments I am making as I return to work.

Work:

Family:

Relationships:

Faith:

Time:

Schedule:

Other:

The top three changes I must make:
-
-
-

People I will share this with:

Anticipate your Return

It is helpful to visualize your first week back at work. Preparing for that now will lighten your reentry process.

Emotions I anticipate experiencing as I return to work and routines...

Challenges I anticipate...

What do I anticipate will be the hardest thing about returning to work?

Why?

> A Prayer for My Return Back to Work

# PART FOUR
The Reorient Phase

The Reorient Phase

"Perhaps nothing in our external circumstances has changed, but we have changed, and that's what our world needs more than anything." [51]
Ruth Haley Barton

Strange things await leaders who return to work from the magical land of sabbatical. Some leaders head back with big expectations to actualize big changes. Others go back hoping to slide back into how they were functioning before sabbatical. You will feel the tension of heading back to the challenges of work with new dreams and ideas. This moment is actually a great time to continue dreaming. Don't let this muscle atrophy; you must continue to use it. In this section I'll walk you through the challenges and opportunities that lie in front of you during your reentry process.

Journal Entry: "My Second Day Back to Work"
Yesterday was a ride. I woke up anxious and stayed anxious most of the morning. I was thinking about the details. "What is going to hit me today?"

My mind said, "Let's go hard", but I had to put a governor on myself. I wanted to get to every detail, text every client and get to the bottom of my inbox. But I worked the plan of gentle reentry.

Hitting the gym was helpful to work out the energy. So was having short meetings. I had asked my team members to respond to just a few questions, and they were kind to not overload me. I got unusually tired from the little amount of work I did. The biggest win was solidifying my new schedule directly from my fresh sabbatical gleanings. I shared it with my team, and they're a go to help me protect it.

At the end of the day I felt discouraged, but nothing was actually discouraging. It was fatigue. I was also grieving that this beautiful time was over.

Gentle Reentry

My kids are tired and grumpy during their first two weeks back to school each fall. They tire quickly, because they're readjusting. It's similar for leaders heading back to work. So much of the secret to healthy reentry lies in pacing yourself. When you're feeling rested, a bit anxious about what challenges await you and a little bit guilty that your team has been working without you, it's easy to dive back in head first. Resist the urge! I challenge leaders to only work at 50% capacity during their first week back, 70% on week two and to land on 80% capacity moving forward.

During your first week back you will be more tired than you imagine. Trust me. Your capacity will be (surprisingly) lower than you think it will be. Your brain will tell you, *"Go for it! Put the pedal to the metal!"*, but you will tire quickly. Entering too quickly can lead to discouragement and even hopelessness. Like a diver going from the depths back to the surface, if you reenter too quickly there can be serious consequences. Lead at half capacity to get you back into the swing of it.

What is my plan for my first week back at 50% capacity?

I encourage leaders to build their second week back to be at 70% capacity. Dial a few more things back up. Ask a little deeper questions with your direct reports, look ahead at the schedule with your team and begin thinking about that upcoming project.

What is my plan for my second week back at 70% capacity?

Holding Space to Lead at 80% Capacity

After your first two weeks back to work you'll begin to normalize. I challenge you not to move beyond 80% capacity right now. It will be tempting, but don't do it. This is valuable for you and those you lead.

Leave 20% of your capacity for fresh ideas. You have fresh dreams, desires and convictions from your time away. If you fill your schedule back up you won't have space to implement that new idea, dream or project you really want to pursue. I've watched God shape and mature leaders during sabbatical. Many leaders hold 20% of their capacity and integrate new ideas and habits into their life. I've also experienced the joy of that myself. If you realize it's time to write the book, develop your staff, launch a new program or pursue more study time, this process provides space to regularly pursue that.

What do I need to create space for in my weekly schedule?

What would I long to do with one whole work day freed up each week?

Let your staff take on extra responsibilities. Your staff has a greater capacity now. After stretching and carrying aspects of your role, their capacity grew. They should continue carrying some of the extra responsibilities they grew into during your sabbatical. Many of those tasks aren't the best use of your time anyway, so it's a win on both sides. During your direct report meetings ask them about how their capacity grew and which of these responsibilities they can carry into the future.

Which of my responsibilities can others take on?

Don't put the unnecessary things back into your schedule. Some of the things you were doing before sabbatical weren't helpful. You emptied the junk drawer of your responsibilities out onto the table, and you realized not everything needs to be placed back into your schedule. Maybe you realized you have crammed way too much into your week, and it's not working well for you. This is a great chance to cut some of those things out.

Which tasks do I need to eliminate from my schedule?

Navigating Meetings With Direct Reports

Everyone seems to fumble for a plan during their reentry. I will get very specific here in order to ease some of your cognitive load. There are several common reactions to leaders returning from sabbatical. Your team may want a formal or informal report on how it went. They may brace themselves, fearing that you're coming back with fifty new ideas to implement. Your direct reports may feel the need to share everything that happened while you were away. I want to guide you with some specific things to do that will ease your reentry process.

Send your direct reports specific questions to answer during your first meeting. Some leaders send these a week before sabbatical ends through an assistant or team member. Keep these questions midlevel and high level, and avoid delving into all the details. You will need to listen to them intently before setting changes into motion. Maybe it was extremely difficult having you away or maybe they rose to a new level of influence and they're feeling confidence. Meet with them to ask specific questions before you make further decisions.

You'll need to put a governor on yourself and resist the urge to know every detail and answer every email immediately. Remind your team that you are easing back in, and you'd like to stick to the questions you sent over. They're also going to want to hear an overview of what you learned and experienced during sabbatical. The exercises you did in the last few weeks of sabbatical can be helpful for sharing with them. Here are some questions I highly recommend for your direct reports.

In what specific areas did you grow while I was away?
What big or small wins did you experience while I was away?
What fears do you have about me returning to work?
How can I help support you in the future?

The Lies About Going Back

You're going to experience some lies rolling around in your heart as you return. While they are slightly different for every leader here are some usual suspects.

You are going to lead exactly how you did before sabbatical. You were brimming with hope just a few days ago, but now you're sure you're going to go back to the level of fatigue or overwhelm you experienced before. You'll be tempted to believe sabbatical was a nice long vacation and you were naive to think your priorities could shift and you can live and lead healthy while you're working.

You can't run like you could before sabbatical. You will likely experience a fear of not being able to hustle or produce like you did before. Your adrenaline levels are down, and you may not feel like gripping work as tightly as you used to. Upon returning from her sabbatical Barton said, "I wondered if I would ever be capable of producing again. I wondered if I would ever even care about producing as much as I had cared about it before."[52] This lie hits almost every leader who returns from sabbatical.

It's impossible to change, so you might as well resign. Many leaders feel stuck when they return. They step back into the routine, the barrage of meetings, the grind of email and the same challenges that slowly eroded their energy before sabbatical. Their conclusion: *the only way to preserve my health is to resign.* This is almost never a good decision, especially the first few weeks back. Don't resign; redesign.

You need to have a huge takeaway to share. Leaders often feel the pressure to have a massive lesson or takeaway to share with their team or congregation when they return. They want others to feel it was worth their time away. If you did the work in the last few weeks to name the things you learned or relearned during sabbatical share some of those. The simple things you learned often reassure your team the most.

What lie am I believing the most as I return from sabbatical?

Redesigning Your Schedule

Most leaders don't need to resign after sabbatical, but every leader can redesign after sabbatical. In your first month back you must translate the internal desires you experienced during sabbatical into external changes in your schedule. This is where sabbatical coaching is hugely helpful. Our coaches help leaders make the changes they desire like spending more relational time with their staff, limiting their meetings, creating more space for deep work, going home earlier or blocking off more space between events.

After one sabbatical I realized I must schedule my exercise like concrete in my calendar or it would get pushed aside. I shifted my work schedule, blocked this off and made sure my team was good with it. My exercise raised my energy levels and increased my productivity.

What specific changes do I need to make to redesign your schedule?

What are the next steps to ensure these changes happen?

Life After Sabbatical

The biggest challenge after sabbatical is settling into a schedule that is sustainable. Many leaders are accustomed to living constantly overwhelmed with bloated schedules, inboxes, and task lists. Their schedules simply aren't sustainable. When there is no margin, the only option is to make the treadmill go faster. While a level of stress brings us to peak performance, too much stress is dangerous. Our bodies aren't meant to live off constant adrenaline pumping through our veins or caffeine shots helping us survive the next meeting.

Leaders, I hate to tell you this, but we're a bit strange. We are people of extremes. We can relish the adrenaline rush of a deadline, feel energized by being behind and prefer busyness to moderation. We normalize overwhelm with phrases like *"riding the rocket," "busting a hump," "running like crazy,"* and *"just trying to keep my head above water"*. We compare notes with other leaders and get the idea that success requires living continually past our limits. This doesn't work as well as we think it does.

When exhaustion overtakes us, we get overwhelmed. We swing the pendulum and quit, hold back, or play small. Sometimes it feels like the only alternative to living overwhelmed is living underwhelmed. In this state we under-live our lives and miss opportunities in front of us. We hold back from making an impact all the while getting a gnawing sense we're wasting our potential.

What if there was another option besides overwhelm or underwhelm? What if we could live whelmed?

> It is, indeed, possible to live and lead whelmed.

It is, indeed, possible to live and lead whelmed. Whelmed leaders look at each week ready to bring their best without pushing past their limits. They know themselves and have learned to leverage their unique design to multiply value to others. But, like many third options, living whelmed feels impossible at first. In moments of stress, our brains corner us into binary choices, "either/or" decisions. It's tempting to feel like we have to be all in or all out. This may require revisiting your fundamental views of work. Perhaps you learned from full-throttle leaders, have used work to self-medicate or worked in dysfunctional cultures. Maybe you've just never seen healthy leadership modeled.

I want to invite you to find a middle gear between sprinting and stalling. This is not a problem to be solved, but a tension to be managed. An effective leader functions at a sustainable pace, and others are looking to them as the pacesetter. It requires discernment each week and each season. Healthy habits are the pathway to this middle ground of living and leading whelmed. Making proactive decisions ahead of time can help you take ground at a sustainable pace.[53]

> What situations tend to push me toward overwhelm?
>
> What situations tend to push me toward underwhelm?
>
> What will I have to resist in order to live whelmed?

Sustaining Change

As the burnout epidemic rages on and overwhelm quietly smolders in Western culture we need to continually implement mechanisms for health and replenishment. Health never sneaks up on us. Healthy leaders fall back on their systems, not their willpower. I write extensively about the obstacles we face, the opportunities we can seize and the shifts healthy leaders must make in my book *AntiBurnout: A Lighter Way to Live and Lead in a Heavy World*. Here are a few areas you must proactively pursue in order to sustain the change you experienced during sabbatical.

Sustainable habits. If you don't translate your sabbatical epiphanies into ongoing habits the moments of space and clarity you experienced during sabbatical will become a distant memory. I encourage every leader who finishes sabbatical to pick up a copy of *The Right Side up Journal* on Amazon and instill proactive habits into daily life. We created this three month journey for leaders to put their habits and decisions in front of them every day.

Leadership Coaching. Leadership challenges will arise after your sabbatical. These can be particularly discouraging when they topple your fresh plans to pursue a healthier way to live and lead. A solid leadership coach will help you put processes in place to play defense and offense, protecting your priorities while taking new ground.

They will help you clarify what feels confusing and forge a path through the wilderness.

Work/rest tension. There is a constant tension between work and rest. It will always be there. It won't magically disappear, and this may always remain a challenge for you to hold this tension. But it's worth fighting for! You'll never handle this perfectly, but if you put the right habits and rhythms in place you can do meaningful work, replenish your reserves and cultivate healthy relationships.

Weekly sabbath. Perhaps the greatest takeaway leaders have after sabbatical is this: *I can experience rest every week.* Experiencing sabbatical in macro helps leaders to zoom in on Sabbath in micro. Sabbatical comes around infrequently, but rest, reconnection and delight are waiting for us every week. Every practice requires practice, including a weekly Sabbath. It will take some time to normalize and operationalize. I've never met a person who took Sabbath seriously and regretted it. Not one.

Mitigating devices. Devices and those who program them will continue to contend for our attention. Phones and computers continue to soak up our mental, physical, emotional and spiritual energy. Wise leaders are not only fighting for their mental health but also for their mental rest. We must fight this unseen battle for freedom in our minds and hearts with both decisions and systems.

Keeping priorities visual. Whether your sabbatical clarified new priorities or solidified old ones, they are there for the taking. Even the best leaders can turn reactive amidst the whirlwind of life, family, leadership and change. In order to guard your priorities you must make them visual. Keep them where you will see them often. Schedule them. Make them regular. If they are priorities to you they are worth protecting.

At Sabbatical Coaching Group we are working to normalize sabbatical so more leaders can experience transformative life change. We desperately need more healthy and high impact leaders who make a massive difference while caring for themselves and those they love. Yes, we believe both are, indeed, possible.

PART FOUR | The Reorient Phase

What next steps will help me sustain the change I experienced during my sabbatical?

Creating a Sabbatical Policy and Program

I need to warn you about an unintended consequence of your sabbatical; others in your organization will want one. They see a few pictures of you relaxing with your family, they feel how grounded you are as you return and they heard your takeaways in the staff meeting. Now they are looking for their own sabbatical.

If you are hoping to create a sabbatical program in your organization it's helpful for the point leader to experience a sabbatical first. This way others know what to expect. Ideally, the point leader experiences the power of sabbatical and realizes it can be an asset to others in the organization.

One of the greatest gifts a leader can give after sabbatical is launching a staff-wide sabbatical program. This is a natural progression: A leader experiences the power of sabbatical and returns thinking, "I would love for everyone in our organization to experience this, too!" Then they work to implement a sabbatical program that cultivates health and longevity throughout the staff.

Sabbaticals are here to stay. We will continue to see an influx of organizations implementing sabbatical programs. Wise organizations will see this as a tool to create a healthy staff culture, raise retention levels and honor God. Healthy organizations will seek new ways to help employees have a deeper and wider life beyond their work, one that allows them space to cultivate a life oriented toward God, love their families well and serve their communities.

Our team at Sabbatical Coaching Group helps large and small organizations create sabbatical policies that are dignifying and equitable to those who serve in an organization. No two organizations are the same, but we walk with organizations as they discern their sabbatical policy. In the next section we will share a few bullet points of that process.

Several years ago our team was invited to help a large organization implement a sustainable sabbatical policy. It was a tricky situation. The point leader had been "put on sabbatical" as a way to correct some behaviors and get him healthy. This had created a wounded sabbatical narrative, so we knew we would be working to rebuild a trust deficit. Instead of something exciting to anticipate some leaders feared their upcoming sabbatical.

Over the next few years we worked shoulder-to-shoulder with their Executive Team to overcome the obstacles and seize the opportunities around sabbatical. We partnered with them to educate the staff about the healthy relationship between hard work and rest, clarify the why behind sabbatical, plan sabbatical schedules wisely, create a policy that fit their culture, seek feedback and tweak the process continually. While there's no perfect sabbatical program, sabbaticals have become a major tool in their battle for organizational health and staff longevity.

Sabbatical programs are a challenge to start, but a massive win for the organizations who implement them. Sabbatical programs become a staff benefit and a cultural differentiator for organizations. A sabbatical policy ensures the privilege of sabbatical moves beyond the senior leader. We help organizations wade through the process of discernment and implementation so sabbatical policies are both wise and generous. Here are some important things to think about when desiring to create a sabbatical policy.

You burn more fuel in takeoff. It requires energy to get this off the ground. It feels like a heavy load to create a sabbatical policy and get it rolling. Don't get discouraged at the initial resistance.

Learn from others. You can learn from other organizations. Look for organizations that are similar in DNA and size, and they will likely share their sabbatical policy with you. Also, our team at Sabbatical Coaching Group is here to share best practices as we help you design and implement this process.

Fair sabbatical doesn't mean everyone receives the same sabbatical. Every role can receive a sabbatical, but not every role receives the same length of sabbatical. Most organizations decide on a tiered sabbatical process that is fairly distributed throughout the organizational chart.

Rotation is wise. Design a policy that spreads out sabbatical over several years. It is a considerable strain on an organization to have multiple leaders gone at the same time. With wise planning you can spread out sabbaticals to have minimal weight on the staff team working back at home.

Consider the right time of year for leaders to be gone. Every industry and organization has a different momentum cycle. It's wise for leaders to go on sabbatical during a lull in momentum. Also, I don't recommend a leader coming back to a massive event or surge in momentum if possible. Three weeks of the gentle boat ramp on the other side of sabbatical is good for both the leader and the organization.

Years of service can be transferred. Many leaders served for years or decades in another organization, but they never experienced a sabbatical. When they come onto your staff they may wonder if they can transfer those years. For example: your policy allows for a sabbatical every seven years. They served as a pastor for sixteen years on another staff and never experienced a sabbatical. I am a big fan of transferring those years and allowing them to receive a sabbatical within a few years on your staff.

Bless as much as possible. Instead of being stingy with sabbaticals, I encourage boards to bless as much as possible with them. Instead of gifting a month sabbatical bump it to six or eight weeks. Instead of giving a small stipend as a financial gift give a large stipend. I realize every organization has limits, but sabbaticals should be viewed as an investment for both the leader and the organization. This leads to extra blessings, not limiting to bare bones. I've yet to meet an organization who has implemented sabbatical in a healthy way and regrets it. Sabbatical becomes a staff attraction tool, health tool and retention tool that breeds long-term health and impact.

Have a small team who is responsible. Once sabbatical is implemented it's easy to lose sight of it. We suggest finding the right person or people to support this process, especially in organizations with more than twenty staff eligible for sabbatical. This should be a staff member or an outside contractor who can give the program ongoing attention and care. They must care deeply about the sabbatical process, because they become a champion of sabbaticals.

Questions to Answer When Creating a Sabbatical Policy

Clarity is vital when creating a sabbatical policy. Don't assume anything as you are creating your sabbatical policy. Here are some questions for the top tiers of your organization to be aligned on when implementing a sabbatical policy.

- *What is the purpose or purposes of a sabbatical?*

- *Who can receive one?*

- *How long will they be?*

- *How often are they eligible?*

- *What resources will we offer?* (finances, coaching funds, therapy funds, etc.)

- *What sabbatical narrative is our staff carrying?* (You might choose to create an anonymous survey to decipher what they would be afraid of or excited for if you offered a sabbatical program.)

- *Who will be the main driver or owner of the sabbatical vision?*

- *Who will administrate sabbatical details?*

- *Are there any times of year that are "no go" sabbatical times?*

- *What do we hope this produces in our culture a decade from now?*

Helpful Resources

Here are some helpful resources we have created to help you continue to contend for greater health and impact.

AntiBurnout: a lighter way to live and lead in a heavy world by Alan Briggs

The Right Side up Journal: a three month journey toward health and impact by Alan Briggs

The Sabbatical Journey: A self guided learning experience to prepare for, experience and reorient from a life changing sabbatical

About Sabbatical Coaching Group

At **Sabbatical Coaching Group**, we walk alongside pastors and non-profit leaders before, during, and after their sabbaticals. We believe rest isn't just about stepping away from work—it's about stepping into renewal. Our coaching process helps leaders prepare with intention, engage sabbatical deeply, and return with clarity. We offer practical tools, honest questions, and relational support to ensure sabbatical isn't just a pause, but a turning point. We want to see leaders—and the people they lead—come back healthier, more aligned, and ready for what's next.

About the Author

Alan Briggs is an adventurer. Whether he is climbing a mountain in the Rockies, guiding a leader through change, hosting conversations about faith around a fire or planning a trip he is committed to continual risk and challenge. By a long shot the greatest adventure in his life is being a husband to Julie and a dad to his four kids.

All of his professional work spins on the axis of cultivating healthy and high impact leaders and organizations. He coaches leaders, trains teams, speaks to hungry groups and hosts leaders in Colorado to restore their vision. visit **www.h2leader.com** to learn more,

Other Books from Far Peak Press

AntiBurnout: We live in a heavy world, and leaders feel the brunt of it. We need practical ways to not only avoid the burnout epidemic, but lead well for the long haul. Leadership Coach, Alan Briggs, shares practical steps and tools to help you avoid burnout and reach more impact that come directly from his coaching experience with leaders across sectors.

Fire Nights: When loneliness is an epidemic and addiction and suicide rates among men are alarmingly high, *Fire Nights* offers a refreshing solution. Burke Atkerson invites you into a transformative experience that challenges the status quo of masculinity, offering a bold, raw, and deeply inspiring response to the crisis of male isolation.

The Superpower Quest: The Superpower Quest is a 5-phase process of self discovery. It's an adventure to discover your special abilities that bring you the most joy, and bring the most impact to the people around you. In this book, you will Discover your Superpower, Steward your Weak Spot, Join Forces, Build Your Utility Belt, and Face Your Supervillain.

The Brand Blueprint: In a world obsessed with algorithms and overnight success, *The Brand Blueprint* offers busy leaders a grounded, human-centered path to building a brand that actually lasts. Whether you're a startup entrepreneur, a small business owner, scaling an organization, or leading a nonprofit initiative, this book delivers practical strategies to clarify your message, grow with purpose, and create sustainable impact—without losing yourself to frustration, overwhelm, or the next guru hack along the way. Coming September 2025. Download a sample at www.brandblueprintbook.com.

Endnotes

PART ONE

1. Richard Foster, Celebration of Discipline (Harper & Row Publishers, 1978), 1.
2. Ruth Haley Barton, Invitation to Solitude and Silence (IVP Books, 2010), 114.
3. D.J. Didona, "The Case for Sabbaticals–And How to Take a Successful One", Harvard Business Review, February 4, 2025.
4. Eugene Peterson, A Long Obedience in the Same Direction (IVP Press, 2000), 25.
5. Alves, David, A Sabbatical Primer (Alves, 2014), 31.
6. Peterson, A Long Obedience (IVP Press, 2000), 15.
7. William Burnett and Dave J. Evans, Designing Your New Life Work (Vintage Books, 2021), 177-219.
8. A.J. Swoboda, Subversive Sabbath (Brazos Press 2018), 52.
9. Archibald D. Hart, The Hidden Link Between Adrenaline and Stress, (Thomas Nelson 1995).
10. Byung-Chul Han, The Burnout Society, trans. Erik Butler, (Stanford University Press 2015).
11. Han, The Burnout Society, trans. Erik Butler, (Stanford University Press 2015).
12. Christina Maslach and Susan E. Jackson, "The Measurement of Experienced Burnout", *Journal of Occupational Behavior* (1981), 99–113.
13. Alison Dubois and Molly Mistretta, Overcoming Burnout and Compassion Fatigue: A Guide for Student Affairs Administrators and Faculty. (Routledge 2022).
14. Alex Soojung-Kim Pang, Rest (Basic Books, 2016).
15. Wes Beavis, Let's Talk About Ministry Burnout: A Proven Research-based Approach to the Wellbeing of Pastors (Powerborn, 2019).
16. Swoboda, Subversive Sabbath, (Brazos Press, 2018), 17.
17. Alan Briggs, Anti-Burnout, (Far Peak Press, 2024), 179-182.
18. Swoboda, Subversive Sabbath (Brazos Press 2018), 5.
19. *Ibid*, 49.
20. Hart, Adrenaline and Stress (Thomas Nelson 1995), xi-xii.
21. *ibid*, 27.
22. *Ibid*, 17, 32-33.
23. Mark Buchanan, The Rest of God (Thomas Nelson 2006), 18.

24 Alan Briggs, host, Jonathan Collier, co-host, *Stay Forth Leadership Podcast*, podcast, "The Expectation Gap: Inner Critics, and Starting the New Year with Curiosity (Part 1 with Steve Cuss)", *January 9, 2025, https://www.podbean.com/ep/pb-u6kks-17a1eb1.*

25 David Alves, A Sabbatical Primer for Pastors (Alves, 2014), xi, xiii.

26 D.J. Didona, "The Case for Sabbaticals—And How to Take a Successful One." Harvard Business Review, February 4, 2025.

27 Susan Ratcliffe, ed., Oxford Essential Quotations, 4 ed. (Oxford University Press, 2016).

28 Saundra Dalton-Smith, Sacred Rest (Faith Words, 2017), 109.

29 Timothy J. Keller, Every Good Endeavor (Viking, 2012).

30 Swoboda, Subversive Sabbath (Brazos Press 2018), 28.

31 Dalton-Smith, Sacred Rest (Faith Words, 2017), 99.

32 *Ibid*, 32.

PART TWO

33 Swoboda, Subversive Sabbath (Brazos Press 2018), 37.

34 Barton, Invitation to Solitude and Silence (IVP Books, 2010), 56.

35 *Ibid*, 72.

36 Steve Cuss, The Expectation Gap, (Zondervan 2024), 30.

PART THREE

37 Saundra Dalton-Smith, Sacred Rest (Faith Words, 2017), 109.

38 Hart, Adrenaline and Stress (Thomas Nelson 1995).

39 *Ibid*, 67.

40 Catherine de Hueck Doherty, Poustinia: Encountering God in Silence, Solitude and Prayer (Combermere, ON: Madonna House Publications, 1993, 2000), 5.

41 Barton, Invitation to Solitude and Silence (IVP Books, 2010), 95.

42 Henri J.M. Nouwen, The Way of the Heart: Connecting with God through Prayer, Wisdom, and Silence (Ballantine Books, 1981), 15–22.

43 Dalton-Smith, Sacred Rest (Faith Words, 2017), 32.

44 Stephen R. Covey, 7 Habits or Highly Effective People: rev. ed. (Simon & Schuster UK, 2020), 33.

45 Alan Briggs, Anti-Burnout, (Far Peak Press, 2024), 77-82.

46 Mark Buchannan, The Rest of God (Thomas Nelson, 2006), 84.

47 Covey, 7 Habits (Simon & Schuster UK, 2020), Habit 3.
48 Briggs, Anti-Burnout, (Far Peak Press, 2024), 205-206.
49 *Ibid*, 51-52.
50 *Ibid*, 52-53.

PART FOUR

51 Barton, Invitation to Solitude and Silence (IVP Books, 2010), 130.
52 *Ibid*, 126.
53 Briggs, Anti-Burnout, (Far Peak Press, 2024), 187-189.

Sources

Alves, David. *A Sabbatical Primer for Pastors*. Alves, 2014.

Barton, Ruth Haley. *Invitation to Solitude and Silence*. 2nd ed. IVP Books, 2010.

Beavis, Wes. *Let's Talk About Ministry Burnout: A Proven Research-based Approach to the Wellbeing of Pastors*. Powerborn, 2019.

Buchanan, Mark. *The Rest of God*. Thomas Nelson, 2006.

Briggs, Alan. Anti-Burnout. Far Peak Press, 2024.

Briggs, Alan, host. Collier, Jonathan, co-host. *Stay Forth Leadership Podcast*. "The Expectation Gap: Inner Critics, and Starting the New Year with Curiosity (Part 1 with Steve Cuss)." January 9, 2025. https://www.podbean.com/ep/pb-u6kks-17a1eb1.

Covey, Stephen. *The 7 Habits of Highly Effective People. rev. ed*. Simon & Schuster UK, 2020.

Cuss, Steve. *The Expectation Gap*. Zondervan, 2024.

Dalton-Smith, Saundra. *Sacred Rest: Recover Your Life, Renew Your Energy, Restore Your Sanity*. FaithWords, 2017.

Didona, D.J. "The Case for Sabbaticals—And How to Take a Successful One." *Harvard Business Review*, February 4, 2025.

Doherty, Catherine de Hueck. 1993. *Poustinia: Encountering God in Silence, Solitude and Prayer*. Madonna House Publications. Reprint, 2000.

Dubois, Alison, and Molly Mistretta. *Overcoming Burnout and Compassion Fatigue: A Guide for Student Affairs Administrators and Faculty*. Routledge, 2022.

Foster, Richard. *Celebration of Discipline*. Harper & Row Publishers, 1978.

Han, Byung-Chul. *The Burnout Society*. Translated by Erik Butler. Stanford University Press, 2015.

Hart, Archibald. *The Hidden Link Between Adrenaline and Stress.* Thomas Nelson 1995.

Keller, Timothy J. *Every Good Endeavor.* Viking, 2012.

Maslach, Christina, and Susan E. Jackson. "The Measurement of Experienced Burnout." *Journal of Occupational Behavior* 2, no. 2 (1981): 99–113.

Milne, A.A. *Winnie-the-Pooh.* With illustrations by E.H. Shepard. Methuen, 1926.

Nouwen, Henri J.M. *The Way of the Heart: Connecting with God through Prayer, Wisdom, and Silence.* Ballantine Books, 1981.

Pang, Alex Soojung-Kim. *Rest: Why You Get More Done When You Work Less.* Basic Books, 2016.

Peterson, Eugene. *A Long Obedience in the Same Direction* (20th Anniversary edition). IVP Press, 2000.

Ratcliffe, Susan, ed. *Oxford Essential Quotations.* 4 ed. Oxford University Press, 2016.

Swoboda, A.J. *Subversive Sabbath.* Brazos Press. 2018.

www.ingramcontent.com/pod-product-compliance
Lightning Source LLC
Chambersburg PA
CBHW020328240426
43665CB00044B/1016